A CASE FOR LEGAL ETHICS

SUNY SERIES IN ETHICAL THEORY
Robert B. Louden, Editor

▼

Recent years have seen a proliferation of work in applied and professional ethics. At the same time, however, serious questions have been raised concerning the very status of morality in contemporary culture and the future of moral theory efforts. Volumes within the SUNY Press Ethical Theory series address the present need for sustained investigations into basic philosophical questions about ethics.

A Case For Legal Ethics

Legal Ethics as a Source for a Universal Ethic

Vincent Luizzi

State University of New York Press

Cover Illustration: VASARELY, Victor. *Ohndo*. 1956–60. Oil on canvas, 7' 2-5/8'' x 71''. Collection, The Museum of Modern Art, New York. Gift of G. David Thompson.

Published by
State University of New York Press, Albany

© 1993   State University of New York

For information, address State University of New York
Press, State University Plaza, Albany, NY 12246

Production by Bernadine Dawes
Marketing by Dana Yanulavich

Library of Congress Cataloging-in-Publication Data

Luizzi, Vincent.
    A case for legal ethics : legal ethics as a source for a universal
ethic / Vincent Luizzi.
        p.   cm. — (SUNY series in ethical theory)
    Includes bibliographical references and index.
    ISBN 0–7914–1271–7 (hard : alk. paper) : $44.50. — ISBN
0–7914–1272–5 (pbk. : alk. paper) : $14.95
        1. Legal ethics.   2. Ethics.   I. Title.   II. Series.
K123.L89   1993
174'.3—dc20
                                                          91–46962
                                                          CIP

10 9 8 7 6 5 4 3 2 1

From their favorite uncle

CONTENTS

FOREWORD

▼

What does it mean to speak of legal ethics or business ethics or military ethics or any other kind of professional ethics? To some it means that the members of a given profession are governed by a special set of moral rules, self-contained and separate from moral principles governing human conduct. The result is typically shallow thinking and shabby conduct.

Take a recent example from the profession of journalism. A newspaper learns that a former tennis star has contracted AIDS. Should they report this fact or keep it confidential? For the editor of *USA Today* the decision was easy and obvious: the information was news, so the newspaper must print it. It wasn't necessary to weigh the likely harm of printing the story against any possible benefits. It wasn't necessary to view the matter from the point of view of the former tennis star. The question of what constitutes news, what is newsworthy, apparently wasn't posed. The right to privacy was apparently not a concern, or no right at all.

Professional ethics cut off from universal moral principles is readily reduced to a few simple admonitions. Moral complexity is averted and moral problems do not arise. So a doctor does not hesitate to use every means at his disposal to extend a terminally ill patient's life, because preserving life is what a doctor is supposed to do. Or a defense lawyer does not hesitate to besmirch the reputation

of the victim of a crime, because a lawyer must do whatever he can
to serve the interests of his client. That one might be acting inhu-
manely or unjustly does not occur to the doctor or the lawyer—they
are simply carrying out their respective professional obligations.
These professional obligations must not be confused with the ordinary obligations that human beings have to one another.

Vincent Luizzi rejects this misguided view of professional
ethics. He recognizes that there cannot be one morality for lawyers,
another for doctors, a third for journalists, and so on. There is only
morality as such, whose fundamental principles underlie the specific
moral rules of the various professions. But how are these rules to be
determined? It is tempting to answer: by deducing them from the
fundamental principles of morality, as the theorems of geometry are
deduced from the axioms. This is not Professor Luizzi's answer.

Focusing on legal ethics, Professor Luizzi argues that the ethical rules governing the conduct of lawyers derive from a conception
of the role of a lawyer and so evolve through critical reflection on
that conception and the rules appropriate to it. This critical reflection is constrained by moral principle: a conception of one's role as a
lawyer is valid only if one—following Kant's principle of universaliz-
ability—would be willing to have others also adopt that conception.
And this mode of ethical thinking, Professor Luizzi argues, is para-
digmatic, not only for the ethics of other professions but for ethics in
general. Every human being occupies various roles, including the
comprehensive role of human being. It is by thinking about these
roles—about what it means to be a parent or a citizen or a neighbor
or a human being—that we develop the rules that define our rights
and obligations and assist us in applying the fundamental moral
principle in our daily lives.

Professor Luizzi articulates this thesis with clarity and defends
it systematically. *A Case for Legal Ethics* can profitably be read not
only by philosophers but also by professors of law and practicing
lawyers—indeed by anyone interested in a thoughtful examination of
the nature of ethical thinking.

John R. Silber

ACKNOWLEDGMENTS

▼

This book has its roots in a number of events that were beginning in
the late 1970s. Fresh out of school in 1976, I was beginning to think
seriously about what I had learned about ethics from my study of
philosophy and law; both fields discussed ethics but neither field
seemed to say much about the other. That was not surprising, since
philosophizing about the professions was just getting under way:
Business and Professional Ethics Journal, now a major journal in
the field, began in 1978 as a newsletter, *Business and Professional
Ethics.* If, figuratively speaking, I was at the frontier of an academic
field, nothing could have been a more literal counterpart in my life
than my trek from law school at Boston University to Southwest
Texas State University for an assistant professorship of philosophy.
The two frontiers converged early on when I was assigned the task
of putting together and teaching Southwest Texas State University's
first course in professional ethics.

The department chair, then Keith Lovin, created an environment in which scholarship was deeply valued. At Lyndon Johnson's
alma mater, that was a Texas size task; because the university styled
itself a teaching institution, we ended up teaching more than most
professors in the country. One of the best things that my colleagues
at SWT did to help my scholarship along was to introduce me to the

New Mexico-West Texas Philosophical Society, the oldest philosophical society in the Southwest. The Society is a model for academic gatherings—a small and congenial group of professionals who assemble yearly to try some new thoughts out on each other. Each year in April as we met sometimes in Santa Fe and Albuquerque, sometimes in Lubbock and El Paso, I took the opportunity to think through and present to the society what I considered to be a major issue in ethics and legal ethics. Presentations I made there, especially "Is Legal Ethics Unique," "Morally Educating our Lawyers," "Pragmatic Ethical Theory," and "Complaints about Moral Philosophy," became cornerstones for much of my thinking in this book.

For over a decade I sought advice from J. M. Orenduff, John R. Silber and the late Michael Bayles about the general direction of my thinking. Bayles insisted that I decide early on where I stood on the debate over the domain of legal and general ethics, and Silber urged that I resolve it in favor of the primacy of a general ethic. Both advised correctly. J. M. Orenduff provided comprehensive support that extended beyond advice on direction to the identification and even creation of opportunities for the development of this book.

Virginia Black, Michael Mitias, and Leo Zonneveld reviewed the entire manuscript. Guided by thier suggestions and support, I wrote the prologue and epilogue.

The Texas Bar Foundation provided support for the critical appraisal, technical editing, and typing of the manuscript; Gerhard Wurzer Gallery of Houston helped fund illustration of the work.

In selecting illustrations, I was assisted and influenced by David Cano, Rick Chafey, Tom Gallaher, Jeffrey Gordon, Robert and Maude Ogle, and Lai Orenduff.

Douglas Anderson edited the manuscript. Jeffrey Gordon and Audrey McKinney stood by to edit and advise me on parts of the manuscript on demand. Joyce Hull typed it. I submitted it to SUNY Press where Carola Sautter, editor, and Bernadine Dawes, production editor, made this experience in publishing a favorite.

Rouault develops his conception of judges in early and later proofs of Judges. © 1992 ARS, N.Y./ADAGP, Paris.

ROUAULT, Gorges. *Juges (Judges).* 1938. Aquatint, undescribed proof before the published edition, printed on wove paper 350 x 250 mm. V. Luizzi Collection, Austin. Gift of Vincent and Elnora Luizzi.

ROUAULT, Gorges. *Juges (Judges)*. 1938. Aquatint, proof before the published edition, printed on wove Montva paper 350 x 250 mm. Collection of Robert Biard, Austin.

Prologue

After reading the manuscript for this book, one of my reviewers sent me a card that he said reminded him of me and my project. It showed a thick forest of elongated silver trees against a pink background. In the midst was a biplane piloted by a fellow wearing goggles and a World War I leather aviator's cap. There seemed to be no question that the plane, which was heading toward the left side of the card, had successfully traversed the forest lying behind it and that the pilot would continue on his journey through the trees. The expression on the pilot's face was nonchalant. The whole thing seemed surreal, quite unusual and unlikely, while at the same time the message was conveyed that we should correct any such impression, since, as a matter of fact, things were going quite well. What is the nature of this unlikely yet viable project that the reviewer thinks I have undertaken?

This is a book about legal ethics and general ethics. It is a book about how all of us can learn something from the pragmatic fashion in which lawyers deal with ethics. It is a book that explores the process of legal ethics to discover a foundation in human nature for both legal and general ethics. And it is a book that demonstrates how this foundation, once it is made explicit, requires us to study in a new light much of the thinking in legal ethics on the nature of professions, the legal profession, the adversary system, and society. This last focus of the book, although of primary interest to those in the field of law, is still relevant for general ethics, since it serves as an example of how all of us are to examine critically our roles and our environments.

What is this desirable process or procedure of legal ethics that I speak of? I observe that legal ethics involves an ongoing process in which lawyers think about how best to conceive of themselves as attorneys and tie rules of conduct to these conceptions. For example, when lawyers thought of themselves not as people in business but as people who were responding to a noble calling of public service, they formulated and observed rules restricting advertising. As they rethought their role, so too did they change the rules governing advertising to accord with the new conception. Notice how the question of whether to advertise is answered by reference to how lawyers conceive of themselves, and notice how that conception is open for evaluation and reevaluation. I see this as a desirable process for all of us to employ in thinking about ourselves and the governance of our conduct.

Think of our various roles, our work and family roles, our roles within clubs, societies, and religious groups, our roles as a friend, neighbor, borrower, lender, adviser, advisee, donor, recipient, patient, client, as a citizen of a city or state, and even as a human. Now think of none of these as fixed conceptions and of each as open for our construction. Think of there being a number of variables to choose from in defining each role and of its being up to us to choose among these variables.

For example, in thinking about being a ruler, one might begin with Machiavelli's famous question about whether it is better to be loved or feared. But do not choose yet. Consider other possibilities for thinking about the chief quality of a ruler in relating to the citizens— possibilities like being trusted, revered, or regarded as amiable. Recognize that the choice guides one's actions as a ruler, leading one to pursue those actions that are conducive to and promote this quality and to avoid those that are not conducive to it or that fail to promote it.

In effect, we are actively constructing our role as a ruler, and this bears directly on how we would conduct ourselves as a ruler. We would continue in this fashion to build our conception of a ruler as we move to other dimensions of the role, such as the educational level of a ruler or the amount of power to be assigned to the ruler. Further, there is an important sense in which our environments are but extensions of our roles and, as such, are subject to the same constructive process. Rulers who choose to think of their being feared by the citizens as part of their role are already shaping the sort of society they rule.

Our willingness for others to imitate us in the roles we construct serves as the check on our constructions and is the point of entry for the moral dimension of this process. In effect, a criterion that demands consistency of action, like the Golden Rule, is operative but which I state in terms that are relevant for this process of constructing roles. We allow ourselves to construct and to act in accord with conceptions of our roles only if we are willing to serve as a role model for others in this regard.

This is a first approximation of the fashion in which the constructive process of legal ethics provides insights that are useful to all of us in thinking about ourselves and our conduct. It is the primary insight for the case that I make for legal ethics as a *source* for a universal ethic; as the work unfolds we will see how the development of a theory that provides the foundation for both legal and general ethics draws on the desirable procedural features of legal ethics that we have discussed.

Most people, I think, are convinced that there is a good case against legal ethics, drawing for support on such popular examples of lawyer misconduct as the fact that lawyers defend the guilty. But even if that sort of case can be made successfully against lawyers, that does not mean that the process or procedure that we attributed to legal ethics is not viable. Put differently, *how* lawyers think about their roles and their conduct can be a good thing regardless of *what* they do. Surely we recognize that, even if there is considerable criminal activity in our democratic society, that does not mean we should abandon the democratic process of lawmaking. Again, those who have a case to make against legal ethics are concerned with actual attorney misconduct and not at all with the procedures that I argue are desirable.

This work cuts against the usual and the familiar both in legal ethics and general ethics. Most works in legal ethics are oriented toward identifying specific ethical issues that the lawyer faces and suggesting how they should be resolved. This work identifies and solves no particular problem in legal ethics but rather makes explicit and justifies the foundation for ongoing analyses of specific issues. It provides a theory of legal ethics. The work also differs from usual contributions to legal ethics because in it I draw widely on a long legacy of ideas and methodologies of general ethical theory that are rarely, if ever, mentioned or employed in works on legal ethics. As for how this work differs from the usual fare in general ethics, it includes a great deal of talk about the legal profession and its ethics, which would not appear in works that are concerned with ethics for everybody.

This study is also significantly different from works that specifically address the relationship between legal ethics and general ethics. As I bring out in the first chapter, all these studies operate from a false assumption that limits the inquiry. They suppose that either general ethics is the primary ethic and lawyers should conform to it, *or* that, because of the special circumstances lawyers are in, they have a special ethics, legal ethics, which sometimes exempts them from the general norms that are binding on the rest of us. This work challenges the assumption that these are the only alternatives for thinking about legal and general ethics by taking seriously the possibility that general ethics should be more like legal ethics and that legal ethics can serve as a model in some ways for general ethics.

To develop the thesis that the approach attorneys take to ethics is a useful one that can advise each of us, it is important to establish that legal ethics indeed has the features that I attribute to it. I do so by providing in chapter 1 many examples of lawyers thinking critically about how best to conceive of their role and many examples of how they tie rules of conduct to these conceptions. The reader who is convinced early on or for whom the matter is already obvious can go on to the next section. Throughout the work I may, in order to establish a claim adequately, offer more documentation than a reader may wish to peruse, and I likewise recommend that that reader turn to the next point in the development of the work.

After offering support for my claim that legal ethics does have the qualities I attribute to it, I focus on how these qualities allow legal ethics to overcome problems associated with some major ethical theories. But knowing what qualities are desirable for ethical theory does not itself an ethical theory make. Preliminary to identifying a uniform theory that will ground both legal and general ethics, I conclude chapter 1 by highlighting the pragmatic nature of the desirable qualities of legal ethics.

In chapter 2 I establish the general theory that incorporates the desirable, procedural aspects of legal ethics. Ultimately, I argue for a theory of human nature that depicts us as *constructors of rule-referring conceptions* of our roles, including our "role" as human beings. I devote some time to distinguishing it from similar views. Further, I here bring in the moral dimension to our formulating conceptions of our roles; I introduce the requirement of our being willing to serve as a role model for all in the various roles we construct. I reserve the full development of this aspect of the theory for chapter 5.

But before addressing the significance of role models for our ethic, I press on in chapters 3 and 4 with how the general theory requires lawyers to recognize alternatives open to them in how they conceive of themselves and their environments. In chapter 3, I survey the substantial literature on the elements of a profession and of law as a profession, and I use this traditional literature to drive home the point that the attorney must resolve many issues in constructing a conception of a professional and of an attorney. This experience of the attorney has relevance for all of us as role constructors, since it demonstrates the nature of the task of thinking critically about and constructing a single role. The same goes for attorneys thinking about their environments or their roles within the context of the adversary system and of society. Chapter 4 focuses on alternatives for thinking about these environments and serves as an example of what goes into constructing conceptions of our contexts or environments.

In chapter 5 I return to the level of general theory and pay special attention to the requirement that we must be willing for others to use us as a role model when we construct roles for ourselves. Although this aspect of our ethical theory places an important restriction on us as role constructors, it also creates opportunities for us for morally educating others and for creating better environments. Because of the significance our universal ethic attaches to the hypothesis of role modeling, I consider ways of establishing the viability of the hypothesis. I bring out, for example, how much of the thinking about moral education has either presupposed some hypothesis about role modeling or how it can be strengthened with such a hypothesis. In effect, support for the validity of this insight about role modeling is provided by the large number of theories that make use of it.

I now invite the reader to step into the plane and share the pilot's role as this intellectual adventure begins.

ROUAULT, Gorges. *Men of Justice.* 1913. © 1992, N.Y./ADAGP, Paris.

1

A Case for Legal Ethics

Little would seem more contrary to common sense than a suggestion that lawyers could have something to teach humanity about ethics. Not unfamiliar are quips that legal ethics is like a square circle; such quips undoubtedly draw on a perception that any group that could engage in such practices as the defense of the guilty, the representation of exploitative businesses, the humiliation of court witnesses, not to mention the deliberate complication for its own pecuniary interests of such simple matters as a house closing, a divorce, or an estate settlement, must quite obviously have few if any concerns with what is ethical.

Nonetheless, it is precisely the thesis of this book that some of the procedural dimensions of legal ethics display very desirable features that provide the contours for general ethics. By attending to these teachings from legal ethics, we are able to derive a general theory of ethics that fundamentally alters how we think about ourselves and our obligations. Also, once made explicit, this general theory rooted in legal ethics in turn allows us to return to legal ethics and enrich and improve that field by bringing legal ethics more in line with its own essence.

Of much concern to moral theorists these days, especially with the proliferation of those who style themselves specialists of legal, medical, and business ethics, is the question of the domain of general ethics and its relationship to these areas of applied ethics. Do principles of general ethics govern universally, so that legal ethics, say, simply represents an application of the basic rules of morality to the particular setting of the attorney? Might not the principle of lawyer-client confidentiality simply be the result of one's applying general utilitarian guidelines requiring the production of the greatest good for the greatest number to the issue of the status of these conversations?; after all, arguably, everyone in society is better off with such a practice. Consider how the lawyer can better help the client who is encouraged to be forthright within the framework of confidentiality. And consider that all citizens of a society can take solace in the thought that, should legal problems arise, they can turn to attorneys as confidants. Or is there something unique about legal ethics, making it quite other than a mere specialized application of general ethics? Arguably, the confidential communications between lawyer and client have no counterpart in general ethics when we consider that within the purview of such communications may be the protection of one who has caused great harm to others. In any case, it is noteworthy that some theorists identify the relationship between general and professional ethics to be the most important issue for professional morality. Against this backdrop, the thesis of this book, that legal ethics provides a good model for general ethics or that general ethics should be more like legal ethics, is a marked departure from the usual fashion of thinking about this issue, and a full consideration of it will pull us in a variety of directions.

THE DEBATE

First, we will consider how the debate over the relationship between general and legal ethics has been staged, and we will show how the possibility of using legal ethics as a paradigm for the development of ethical theory has been obscured. We consider seriously the case that can be made for legal ethics occupying this role and find that it hinges on legal ethics being pragmatic in nature. A summary of the debate over whether legal ethics is "unique" as against general morality follows. It should be mentioned that this characterization of the debate is borrowed from one of the commentators[1] and that admittedly some infelicities surround such a description; as will become apparent, many theorists are puzzling over the similarities and differences of these ethics and are not always prepared to conclude that one is unique or both are congruent. With these qualifications, let us turn to a sketch of those arguments purporting to show that legal ethics is "unique":

1. The attorney operates within the adversary system of justice, which permits such actions as withholding information, defending those who have confessed to crimes, and discrediting and humiliating witnesses, all to further the client's cause and all of which is beyond the purview of ordinary morality.[2]

2. The attorney gives special consideration to the affairs of another, the client, and thus departs from the demands of ordinary morality that require equal treatment of others.[3]

3. The large number of extant professional codes—codes for accountants, for medical doctors, for journalists, and so on—suggests that specialized bodies of ethics are required to handle moral problems peculiar to the respective professions, the legal profession included.

4. Further, each professional code, including the lawyer's code, contains directives that simply do not apply to the ordinary person and are not derivable from the standards of ordinary morality. For example, ethical advice to attorneys concerning their obligation to reveal to the court precedent adverse to their clients neither applies to nor has a counterpart for the ordinary person.

5. "legal ethics centers about the problem of how to secure a larger income for lawyers. The announced precepts of legal ethics have little to do with the basic values of life or with the basic problems of the present social order."[4] Because of this divergence, we must recognize the distinctness of legal ethics from general ethics.

6. A distinguishing feature of professionals, and thus of attorneys, is that they have a moral commitment to meet human needs and a special capacity for doing so. People in need come to professionals for assistance; herein lies the ground for the moral commitment, presumably not just some general, moral prescription to help the needy but one that is tied to the "knowledge resources" that professionals alone have at their disposal that allow them peculiarly to meet these needs.[5]

7. Although the attorney and the ordinary person share the same basic values, there are some, like confidentiality, to which the attorney is more committed and by which the attorney is more constrained. Ultimately, attorneys are not as free to complicate their worlds as the ordinary person is. More concretely, ordinary people are free to agree to keep confidential certain communications and in so doing to complicate their moral worlds as they like. But, unless they choose to do so, they are unfettered in this regard and their moral world is not complicated. Attorneys, on the other hand, do not have this latitude in their communications with their clients. Their moral world is one where such communications are already understood to be confidential, and in this way the attorney's moral world is already complicated.[6]

8. Legal ethics has a formal system for detecting violations of standards, for holding hearings on alleged violations, and for administering punishment, all of which ordinary morality is without. For example, in New York, a Grievance Committee of the Bar Association looks into complaints of attorney misconduct. The Grievance Committee determines whether to bring charges against the attorney, and, if it does so, the matter goes to the state's Appellate Division during one of its Special Terms. The court issues its findings and may, on the basis of the findings, prescribe punishment.[7] Ordinary or customary morality has no such mechanism. One's outrage for another's moral transgressions may find expression in words or actions aimed directly at the scoundrel or in attempts to induce others to join in the condemnation. One may go to particular people in the community known to be quick to become morally outraged and

willing to participate in some campaign of ignoring, insulting, or excluding the culprit. But again, this is all done informally, whereas it is quite otherwise with legal ethics. Indeed, in identifying ways in which pleasure and pain may come to people as sanctions, the utilitarian Jeremy Bentham speaks of "moral or popular sanction" as being "at the hands of...*chance* persons in the community, as the party in question may happen in the course of his life to have concerns with, according to each man's spontaneous disposition, and not according to any settled or concerted rule."[8]

9. The ethics of the attorney is the law, while this is not the case with the ethics of the ordinary person.[9] The idea here is that the codes of professional ethics that lawyers are to follow are usually promulgated by the supreme court of the state within which the lawyer practices. As such, these rules have the status of law. While the moral norms of a community (against stealing and murdering, for example) may be articulated in some of the laws, these moral norms are neither congruent with nor simply a subset of the legal norms. The common moral dictate to do good for others, for example, basically resists any backing from the legal realm.

10. Attorneys have responsibilities to persons and entities—their clientele, their profession, the public—which are not commanded by ordinary morality.[10] As regards the clientele, there is a special fiduciary duty to care for the interests of the client given the possibilities for abuse open to the professional. To the profession are owed duties to comply with and enforce the code of ethics and to render services to the poor. And to the public is the special duty to be a leader in the framing of public issues and in the development of public opinion.[11]

11. While ordinary ethics deals with one person's obligations to another, professional ethics deals with groups, like lawyers, and with obligations to those outside the group.[12] Thus, it would seem quite natural to find one saying, "Those of us who are lawyers should make sure that we act thusly when we come in contact with non-lawyers." But on this line of reasoning, it would seem quite odd to find one saying, "Those of us who are humans should make sure that we act thusly when we come in contact with nonhumans."

Let us now turn to arguments on the other side of the debate over the issue of whether legal ethics is unique:

1. Morality basically involves an experimental development of a role and a working out of how one's role governs one's actions. So, although a lawyer's role differs from the roles of others in society and may specify actions different from those specified by the roles of others, the dynamics involved are essentially the same.[13]

2. Despite the variety of regulations in professional codes, one must grant, upon reflection, that the ultimate justification of these are basic, universal principles embracing concepts of justice and utility, such principles being the foundation of any morality.[14] One text on legal ethics begins the chapter "Conflict of Interest" with wisdom from Matthew 6:24: "No man can serve two masters: for either he will hate the one and love the other; or else he will hold to the one, and despise the other: Ye cannot serve God and mammon."[15] No further mention is made of the quotation as the authors go on to detail the ways in which conflicts of interest arise in lawyering and the types of restriction lawyers have placed on themselves. But the inference is an obvious one—there is something we all acknowledge to be wrong with placing ourselves in compromising situations where interests are likely to conflict, and the forbearance of lawyers in this regard is but an instance of what we all try to avoid generally. Put slightly differently, "the different codes of professional groups represent...the deliberate application of a generally accepted social standard to particular spheres of conduct.... What is universal is the good in view, and ethical rules are but the generally approved ways of preserving it."[16] The approach here seems to be one of asserting the pervasiveness of general principles of ethics with the suggestion that the reflective person will either see the truth of this assertion or be hard put to find any counter-evidence to it.

3. Now, if we do not grant what seems obvious in (2) above, ill consequences obtain, and this speaks further for our endorsing (2). More specifically, if professionals conceive of themselves as having a special ethics, they may all too easily begin to think true the faulty

view that "expertise about the technical facts of a given area also gives one expertise in the evaluative factor required for decision-making in that area."[17] And this assumption of evaluative expertise can lead to attorneys excluding their clients from participating in making value judgments. Suppose, for example, your client has been charged with first-degree murder. You have been led to believe by the prosecuting attorney that the state would reduce the charge to negligent homicide in exchange for a guilty plea from your client. An obvious alternative would be for your client to stand trial and strive to be exonerated from any wrongdoing. There is evidently present here a choice that needs to be made, and in part it involves a choice among competing values, one involving the certainty of a lesser sentence and the other involving the possibility of exoneration tied to the risk of a much heftier sentence. There is nothing, in principle, that makes you as an attorney who is particularly skilled in handling legal transactions better able to make this choice among competing values than your client. But you may have been duped into thinking that yours would be the better view in matters of ethics and values that are related to legal transactions from the fact that you, as an attorney, think of yourself as having a special ethics, one different from the ordinary person's. And this claim to a special ethics may have led you to think it perfectly appropriate simply to announce to your client what course of action *must* be undertaken, based on the choice that you would have made. To the extent that excluding clients from decisions important to them is a bad thing, we should endorse as correct the view that precludes such happenings, the view that professional ethics is not a special ethics.

OBSERVATIONS ABOUT THE DEBATE

With this delineation of the contours of the debate, let us make first some general observations and then turn to their significance for resolving the issue. To begin with, we should note that some of the arguments above deal with empirical matters—how things are—others, with normative matters—how things ought to be. More specifically, legal ethics is sometimes contrasted with ethics generally with an observation simply that this is how the one is, that is how the other is. At other times legal ethics is compared with general ethics in order to show what legal ethics should be. So, just looking at the debate, we can recognize that possibilities for analysis include whether or not legal ethics varies or differs from general ethics and, if it does, whether it should.

But more possibilities for analysis become evident upon our recognizing that there is an ambiguity in the phrase "general ethics" that we have been employing. Sometimes it appears that the phrase refers to customary, ordinary, or unreflective morality. At other times the reference seems to be to reflective or critical morality. This contrast between customary and critical morality, of course, strikes up the difference between moral standards that are considered correct because they are accepted by the community and those that are considered correct (even when they diverge from the morals of the community) because they are the product of rational inquiry. With this distinction in mind, we can characterize further the inquiries mentioned above regarding the descriptive and normative relationships between legal ethics and general ethics, depending on how we read "general ethics."

Recognizing all these possibilities for constructing the inquiry, we can see that the debate has focused on two of the possible questions, asking either "Is legal ethics unique or different in relation to customary or critical morals?" or, "Is legal ethics, or should it be considered, nothing more than a part of customary or critical morals?" Now it may be that some of the paths of inquiry have not even a *prima facie* claim of being worthy of pursuit. But there is one path upon which no light has yet been shed and which does, upon analysis, appear to be quite fruitful. I speak here of the possibility that critical or ordinary morality should be more like legal ethics, or, put in terms of inquiries, the question is here raised of whether critical or ordinary morality should be more like legal ethics.

As we brought out above, the possibility of an affirmative answer is counter-intuitive, and the question itself seems pointless given the extent to which many of the practices of attorneys seem to offend the moral sensibility of the community. But regardless of a prejudice even of this sort, the point, whether considered cogent or not, has probably had little chance to surface because of the almost universal assumption that customary or reflective ethics is the primary mode and legal ethics is a unique (or essentially different) yet restricted ethics. Perhaps the sheer numbers to which general ethics applies have obscured the possibility of seeing legal ethics as in some way a paradigm for general ethics. Whatever the explanation is, it is now time to consider what sort of a case might be made for this claim and the extent to which, if it does have merit, we can glean something of significance for the development of ethical theory.

THE CASE FOR LEGAL ETHICS: ITS EMERGING NATURE

Let us distinguish between substantive legal ethics, the specific rules that guide lawyers, and procedural legal ethics, the development of these rules. It is the latter, the process of legal ethics, which we are exploring as a model for general ethics. Usually, I think it will be clear in what follows whether I am referring to procedural or substantive legal ethics if I speak simply of legal ethics. What we can summarily say of procedural legal ethics that captures its essence and at the same time provides the ground for its being a model for ethics is that *the substantive rules of legal ethics emerge from a critically reflective process of assessing what rules best structure the lawyer's experience and guide in the resolution of recurring problems by attending to both what the distinguishing features of attorneys are and what they should be.*

Let us begin to develop this claim by turning first to the recurring problems of lawyers. Our general sense of what the lawyer's problem areas are is confirmed by what we find basically to be the subject matter of the current *Model Rules of Professional Responsi-*

bility of the American Bar Association, of its predecessors, the *Model Code of Professional Responsibility* and the *Canons of Professional Ethics*, of texts on legal ethics, and of articles on legal ethics in journals and law reviews—concerns over conflicts of interests, zealous advocacy, the search for truth, confidentiality, and how to make services available. As regards the manner of dealing with these matters, we find typically that legal ethics operates with a spirit in which the extant solutions to problems are subject to critical reevaluation and change in an ongoing and visible process that unfolds in lay journals and books, law reviews, opinions of courts, bar journals, and meetings of professional associations, all of which we might think of as the community of discourse within which legal ethics unfolds.

Specific examples of this rethinking of issues are readily available, and I offer here a few for illustrative purposes. Judge Marvin Frankel complains in the *University of Pennsylvania Law Review* that the lawyers' *Code of Professional Responsibility* ranks the pursuit of truth too low as evidenced by the fact that various prohibitions, like that against the knowing use of perjured testimony, come under the general dictate advising zealous representation within the bounds of the law, and others, like that against fraud, fall under a heading, "Duty of the Lawyer to the Adversary System of Justice." He suggests revisions that amount to a new rule requiring the disclosure of material facts.[18] Consider, as another example, how the United States Supreme Court in *Bates* rethought the longstanding restriction on lawyer advertising and decided to permit advertising under certain circumstances.[19]

In 1964 Justice Lewis F. Powell, then the ABA's President, called for a committee to review the *Canons of Professional Ethics*. In his statement is evident a spirit of revising for the better the aspects of the Canons that experience has proved to be inadequate:

> Many aspects of the practice of law have changed drastically since 1908. An American Bar Foundation Study Committee has said that these changes make unreliable many of the assumptions upon which the Canons were originally based. As

remarkably flexible and useful as the Canons have proved to be, they need to be reexamined as guidelines for the practicing lawyer. They also should be reexamined particularly in view of the increased recognition of the public responsibility of our profession.[20]

In 1969 the rules and revisions suggested by the new committee were adopted by the ABA as its *Code of Professional Responsibility*.

Also noteworthy for establishing our claim about the emerging nature of legal ethics is the sequence of events leading to the American Bar Association's adoption of its current *Model Rules of Professional Conduct* in 1983; a majority of the states have, by the way, adopted this work in some form. The others mostly subscribe to some form of the ABA's *Model Code of Professional Responsibility*. The American Bar Association's Commission on Evaluation of Professional Standards in 1981 issued the product that resulted from the commission's being "charged with undertaking a comprehensive rethinking of the ethical premises and problems of the profession of law."[21] The chair of the committee described the process in this way: "From the outset, our sessions were drafting sessions, not forums for free-floating debates. Ideas and their consequences had to be tested on paper. In the nature of things, many proposals and approaches to the issues failed this test. Many more, after being subjected to repeated reworking, survived—often substantially altered from the original form in which they were proposed. The process of revision was continuous."[22] Possibilities for revisions ranged from placing limitations on an attorney's ability to breach confidentiality regarding a client's intent to commit a crime to requiring *pro bono* work of attorneys.

Watch how, in proposing some changes to the lawyer's charge to advocate with zeal, the committee makes clear that thinking on the issue has been ongoing and that the current language of rule 1.3 of the *Model Rules,* directing that "a lawyer shall act with reasonable diligence and promptness in representing a client," has emerged through this process of critical evaluation and reevaluation. ("EC" refers to an ethical consideration of the *Model Code*; an ethical consideration sets out advice described as aspirational in nature. "DR" refers to a disciplinary rule of the *Model Code*. The violation of a disciplinary rule by a lawyer could result in disciplinary action; in this sense the advice is considered mandatory.)

A lawyer's duty to act diligently in a client's behalf is part of a general obligation of loyalty to the client. *See* Greene v. Greene, 47 N.Y. 2d 447, 391 N.E.2d 1355, 418 N.Y.S.2d 379 (1979). *See also* ABA Formal Opinion 132 (1935) (Canon 6 of Canons of Professional Ethics prohibits any representation 'where self-interest tempts [the attorney] to do less than his best for his client.'); *ABA CANONS OF PROFESSIONAL ETHICS*, Canon 6 (undivided fidelity). Under the Code, this duty is expressed as acting with 'zeal.' Canon 7; EC 7–1; DR 7–101. The term first appeared in the profession's formal standards of conduct in the ABA Canons of Professional Ethics, Canon 15, which stated in part: 'The lawyer owes entire devotion to the interest of the client, warm zeal in the maintenance and defense of his rights and the exertion of his utmost learning and ability, to the end that nothing be taken or be withheld from him, save by the rules of law, legally applied. Phrasing the duty of loyalty in this way, however, could be construed as requiring a lawyer to invest emotion or personal belief in the client's cause, a meaning clearly not intended. *See, e.g.,* United States v. Landes, 97 F. 2d 378 (2d Cir. 1938); Lucas v. Ludwig, 313 So. 2d 12 (La. Ct. App. 1975); EC7–8; EC7–10; EC7–14; EC7–17; EC7–25; EC7–37–EC739; *ABA CANONS OF PROFESSIONAL ETHICS*, Canons 15, 17 & 18. *See also* Tool Research & Eng'r. Corp. v. Henigson, 46 Cal. App. 3d 675, 120 Cal Reptr 291 (1975). Furthermore, 'zeal' suggests a frame of mind appropriate in advocacy but not ordinarily appropriate in advising a client.

The duty is better conceived as one of commitment to achievement of the client's lawful objective. In this regard the lawyer must act vigorously, not indifferently, in behalf of his client in attempting to secure the client's legitimate objectives. *See, e.g.,* In re McConnell, 370 U.S. (1962).[23]

Another good example of the emerging nature of legal ethics comes from recent thought about the predictable difficulty that can arise from assigning lawyers general obligations to be candid with tribunals and at the same time to be vigilant in preserving the confidences of their clients. Almost a quarter of a century ago, Professor Monroe Freedman offered a resolution to the matter in a fashion that, in the ensuing years, seems especially to have provoked much thought and criticism in the attempt to deal best with the problem. Freedman took an extreme position by reasoning to an affirmative answer to what he sees as "three of the most difficult issues in this general area," including whether it is proper to discredit adverse witnesses that the attorney knows to be truthful, to allow his or her client to take the stand knowing the client will offer perjured testimony, and to give clients legal advice that would tempt the client to commit perjury.[24]

Thought on how lawyers should meet their obligations to be candid with the court and to preserve client confidences has gone in a variety of directions since Freedman's contribution. This thought has led to the following conclusions, each of which further supports our observation about the ongoing assessment that is characteristic of legal ethics: (1) that the lawyer should, in the face of representing a client about to commit perjury, try to withdraw from the case,[25] (2) that the lawyer unsuccessful in withdrawing should allow the client to make a statement but not comment on it to the jury,[26] (3) that lawyers should tell their clients at the outset that a communication about an intent to testify falsely would fall outside the scope of the attorney-client privilege,[27] (4) that lawyers should reveal frauds perpetrated upon people and tribunals unless they are privileged,[28] and (5) that lawyers should not offer evidence known to be false but, if lawyers learn that such has occurred, they should take reasonable steps to correct the record even if the execution of this obligation requires disclosing a confidential communication.[29] Further, in *Nix v. Whiteside* the U.S. Supreme Court held that the Sixth Amendment right of a criminal defendant to the assistance of counsel is not violated if the attorney refuses to assist the defendant in committing perjury. Making reference to both the Model Code and the Model Rules, the Court brought out that "these standards confirm that the legal profession has accepted that an attorney's ethical duty to advance the interests of his client is limited by an equally solemn duty to comply with the law and standards of professional conduct; it specifically ensures that the client may not use false evidence. This special duty of an attorney to prevent and disclose frauds upon the court derives from the recognition that perjury is as much a crime as tampering with witnesses or jurors by way of promises and threats, and undermines the administration of justice."[30] One follow-up to the Court's thinking can be found in a "Formal Opinion" of the ABA, where it was brought out that some states may have constitutional requirements that prohibit the disclosure the U. S. Supreme Court spoke of and that would control the lawyer's conduct.[31]

For further illustration of our claim about the desirable features of legal ethics, let us now turn from the first part of our claim, concerning its developing in a critically reflective fashion, to the second, concerning how rules for conduct are tied to conceptions of attorneys that result from this process. It is worth noting that most of what I cite to support the second part of the claim can also be seen as support for the first, for these varying conceptions of the lawyer's role are the result of the ongoing process of critical assessment and reassessment I have been referring to. So, in effect, more evidence is offered for the first part of the claim as we develop the second.

An example of how both might be illustrated with a single case is Hazard and Rhode's presentation in a recent text of thought about the role of the lawyer as partisan advocate within the criminal defense paradigm, about the way thinking on that role has developed when the paradigm is extended to advocacy in civil contexts, and about ways in which the general role might be reconceived. Considering the role of advocate within the criminal defense paradigm, some say that lawyers must defend clients they know to be guilty lest lawyers take on the role of judge and jury.[32] Considering the role of advocate in civil contexts, some, like Hazard himself, bring out that the obligation shifts: "It is perfectly possible to think that the lawyer for the criminal accused is not 'responsible' for him, while at the same time thinking that the general counsel for a corporation or agency is, in some sense of the word, 'responsible' for it. The point is made by suggesting that it is one thing to represent a sometime murderer, quite another to be on retainer to the Mafia."[33] And some of the thinking that directs our attention to the advocate's obligation to "adopt as his dominant purpose the furthering of his client's interests"[34] grounds this rule of conduct in a rethought role of the lawyer as being like a friend to the client.

Let us go on to consider further that part of our claim about the desirable qualities of legal ethics—that there seems to be a clear link between the thinking about what attorneys are and how they should be conceived, on the one hand, and the thinking about what rules they should follow, on the other. We find that as the conception changes, so too do the rules of conduct. For example, much criticism of the *Code of Professional Responsibility* centered on its embracing a Victorian conception of the lawyer in which the lawyer encounters a client as a discrete entity. Geoffrey Hazard brought out how, in modern times, an enriched notion of the attorney takes cognizance of the fact that some attorneys may have no clients at all; they may, for example, be employed to draft regulations for a government agency. Or, looked at from another perspective, the question of who the client is may have no obvious answer in modern contexts; does the attorney for a corporation have as his or her client the chair of the board, the stockholders, or the directors?[35] The suggestion was that the extant guidelines let us down because the conception of the attorney was antiquated and that better rules would be forthcoming with a revised conception of the attorney.

Most recently, David Luban attempts to build a notion of the lawyer as a moral activist, a notion that would rule out an attorney's engaging in activity such as freeing a rapist on a technicality, activity that Luban thinks objectionable but allowable when we conceive of the attorney as a zealous advocate.[36] And Elliot D. Cohen does much the same with his analysis of the lawyer as "pure legal advocate" versus the "moral agent concept" of the lawyer. The latter, for example, would enable us to rule out activity allowed by the former concept (like advocates saying nothing to the court about their clients having lied to the court).[37]

Further, we find throughout the *Model Rules* and the *Code* a number of phrases characterizing the lawyer as a certain type of person or as having a certain type of role, each carrying with it its own normative advice. We find the lawyer depicted as a guardian of the law,[38] as a fiduciary,[39] as an advocate, as an adviser,[40] as a representative, negotiator, intermediary, evaluator, and public citizen,[41] as well as a couple of roles the lawyer may step into, including that of the legislator or other holder of public office. Thus, we find that it is through the conception of the lawyer qua fiduciary and adviser that we locate the obligation of the attorney to "preserve the secrets and confidences of a client" as prescribed by canon 4 of the *Code* and as adviser and fiduciary that we locate the obligation not to "reveal information relating to the representation of a client" under 1.6 of the *Model Rules*.[42]

Aronson et al., in chapter 7 of their *Professional Responsibility*, present materials for consideration of the lawyer's role as advocate. Included are nineteen opinions of federal and state courts along with the description of, or a quotation from, an additional fifty-five. Here one sees the give and take in the dialogue over how best to conceive of this role and the guidelines tied to it in such matters as when lawyers' claims and defenses are frivolous, when, if at all, lawyers may communicate with adverse parties, jurors, and judges, and when they should disclose adverse facts and legal authority.[43]

The *Lawyering Process: Ethics and Professional Responsibility* presents materials depicting ways of thinking about lawyers as interviewers, investigators, negotiators, presenters of evidence, arguers, and counselors.[44] Each way of thinking informs lawyers about how they should act. The notion of attorneys as interviewers suggests that they are to facilitate communication but to do so in a fashion that does not encourage the fabrication of evidence.[45] The editors reject the standard way of grounding this advice, which portrays attorneys as needing to subordinate their interests to those of their clients in order to create the trust necessary for the relationship. They say that, because attorneys evidently have other loyalties, they may well promote feelings of mistrust if they claim, in the face of this, to act in this subordinate fashion. The suggestion boils down to tying the normative advice about facilitating communication to a better-conceived notion of the attorney as interviewer, one emphasizing "more mutuality and involvement between lawyer and client" rather than client autonomy and lawyer subordination.[46]

In *The Social Responsibilities of Lawyers*, the authors identify many of the social responsibilities by attending to the following "lawyer roles": lawyers for a political movement, lawyers for ordinary people, lawyers for criminal defendants, lawyers for Wall Street, and lawyers for government. Regarding the role of lawyers for a political movement, the authors quote from the analysis of Gary Bellows. Bellows shows the shortcomings of conceiving of the role on a "service model," by which access of the poor to the legal system is primary, and of conceiving of the role on a "law reform model," by which test cases become a primary mechanism for effecting changes in laws for the benefit of the poor. The conception that is superior, according to Bellows, is one in which legal services are seen as an arm of the community organization; that is, the lawyer is to function as part of a political effort, at times as a lawyer, at times as an organizer, an educator, teacher, and PR man.[47] So conceived, the lawyer for a political movement takes on these duties: "He will spend a great deal more time in political organizing, in working on cases and priorities that reflect the group demands of his clients and in developing cases in a way which reinforces their political integration and cohesion."[48]

Professors Sutton and Dzienkowski consider lawyers in the roles of agent, fiduciary, trustee, advocate, negotiator, lobbyist, adviser/counselor, public leader, and intermediary; in each case an effort is made to suggest how these roles carry with them certain obligations for the attorney. Some of the duties carry through the differing roles, like that of loyalty to the client and the preservation of independent judgment by eschewing the representation of parties with conflicting interests. Others, like that of restraining zeal in advocacy to prevent perpetrating a fraud upon the finder of fact and law, are more specifically tied to the well-conceived notion of the lawyer as advocate.[49]

One text on legal ethics, *Becoming a Lawyer: A Humanistic Perspective on Legal Education and Professionalism*, expresses concern about lawyers' being trained in skills of analysis and advocacy with objectivity being a prominent value and all of this figuring centrally in the lawyer's conception of self. The text is replete with selections and comments by the editors intended to assist lawyers in integrating their professional experience with their own human values.[50] In effect, lawyers and law students are invited constantly to think of themselves as humans in whatever they do, and with these reminders come suggestions for how they should act. One selection, for example, sizes humans up as "positive, constructive, moving toward self-actualization, growing toward maturity, growing toward socialization."[51] The editorial comment suggests that the alternative is to embrace a Hobbesian view of human nature that depicts us as competitive, self-interested, aggressive, and always disposed to engage in combat rather than to seek peaceful resolutions to difficulties. The editors' endorsement of the former view is an obvious attempt to encourage law students and lawyers to see themselves and others more as positive beings, a conception that brings with it the advice for lawyers to temper their views of themselves as analytical advocates battling against the opposing side.[52]

In another selection from that text, one of the authors recounts his feelings of fear and inadequacy when he was first placed in the intimidating environment of a classroom full of first-year law students, all seemingly smarter than he, with a professor bent on demonstrating this inadequacy to each student in the class. The author's response was to withdraw for a month and say nothing in the classroom. In the editorial comment that follows, an effort is made to place this experience in the context of situations that are generally fearful to humans, to help the law student and the lawyer see the experience of inadequacy as something that happens not just to them. The analysis continues to recommend that, when we find ourselves in such situations, we should overcome the urge to with-draw (or take measures designed merely to help us feel safe in the face of danger) and rather take on a "broad vision" of the matter.[53] In short, the advice of not withdrawing makes sense when lawyers broaden their conception of appropriate responses for lawyers to include general human responses.

This completes our study of how legal ethics ties advice for attorneys' conduct to conceptions of attorneys. We identified this connection as a part of the ongoing and critically reflective process that assesses how best to conceive of attorneys in their various roles. The many examples we considered amply demonstrate that these characteristics belong to legal ethics. Some people may see this approach to ethics as desirable simply from the foregoing account which shows it to be an approach that keeps our inquiry going and that is experimental, flexible, and critical. In the next section, we will build on these grounds for seeing legal ethics as a model as we explore how legal ethics can overcome problems that other basic approaches to ethics encounter.

First, a disclaimer is in order. While the claim here is that legal ethics displays the desirable qualities mentioned above, it is not important to our case to establish that legal ethics uniquely displays them; I don't rule out the possibility that similar features can be fac-tored out of other areas of applied ethics. Indeed, I think that current opinion favors piecemeal analysis of contemporary moral problems as a way to contribute in an ongoing fashion to our understanding of and dealing with them. But the notion of there being a climate of opinion that guides people's theorizing is hard to tie down, and accordingly, anything we could say about it would be far less exact than what we have been able to observe about legal ethics. The gain in exactness in itself is a good reason for looking at these qualities within the context of legal ethics where its process and those employing it seem far more self-conscious and deliberate than in other branches of applied ethics.

Next, returning to the argument that legal ethics has desirable qualities, it is noteworthy that one of these qualities, the emerging nature of legal ethics, mirrors in many ways the legal process, a process which some already recognize as effective. That legal ethics bears strong resemblance to the legal process should come as no surprise when we consider the considerable similarities between an ethical and a legal system and the extent to which it is likely that lawyers adept in the ways of the law would use the legal process as a reference point for formulating their ethics. It is evident that ethics and law both aim to structure and guide conduct with rules, to promote harmonious and just relations among members of some group or society, and to give some ground for the evaluation of conduct as right or wrong, whether legally or ethically.

Further, lawyers and judges find commonplace in their experience a case law that develops as judges, through the urging of counsel, reshape or create legal rules in an ongoing attempt to effect viable solutions to the legal problems at hand. The well-known history of the development of a single rule in the law of products liability dramatically illustrates the workings of the legal process. Here we see the courts moving from a point where those who did not purchase but were injured by products enjoyed virtually no legal protection, except when the product was probably dangerous, to a point where obligations were placed on the seller and remedies did become available to these persons. According to Edward Levi, we find in *MacPherson v. Buick* that "the exception in favor of liability for negligence where the instrument is probably dangerous has swallowed up the purported rule that 'a manufacturer or supplier is never liable for negligence to a remote vendee.' The exception now seems to have the same certainty the rule once had. The exception is now a general principle of liability...."[54] And Dworkin cites *Riggs v. Palmer* as providing a good illustration of how a court creates a new rule from a preexisting principle and thereby contributes to the emerging character of law. In this case, the question was whether one could inherit from one's grandfather as per the terms of the grandfather's will if one had murdered the grandfather. The court acknowledged that a literal reading of the existing statutes permitted this. But the court drew on a long-standing principle of the common law, that none may profit from their wrongs, to keep the inheritance from going through, and, in so doing, provided case law, and a new rule for decision in future, similar cases.[55]

In a more recent work, Dworkin compares the work of judges in their development of the law to the situation of a number of different writers collaborating on a literary work and in so doing gives us additional insight into the emerging nature of the law. We are asked to imagine one writer composing the first chapter of a novel and sending it to another who will write the second, and so on. Dworkin brings out how each writer, except the first, is faced not just with the task of creating a chapter but of interpreting the entire corpus "to establish...what the novel so far created is."[56] The analog for law is judges deciding hard cases, especially when a judge must determine what rules or principles "underlie" cases related to the instant case. Here the judge "*must* interpret what has gone before because he has a responsibility to advance the enterprise before him rather than strike out in some new direction of his own."[57] Understanding the legal process in this way shows it unmistakably to have an emerging nature much like that of legal ethics. To the extent one sees this emerging quality of the legal system as desirable, one finds support for its counterpart in legal ethics being desirable.

THE CASE FOR LEGAL ETHICS: IT AVOIDS DIFFICULTIES INHERENT IN TRADITIONAL APPROACHES

Regardless of whether one sees the emerging nature of legal ethics as desirable in and of itself, and regardless of whether we can establish its having roots in a desirable legal process, it still remains that, as compared with other major attempts in ethics, its developmental nature allows it to overcome important difficulties traditionally associated with them. To illustrate this, let us consider two major systems of ethics, Kantianism and utilitarianism, each of which is based on a single standard by reference to which we are to make all of our determinations of moral right and wrong. As we will see, each, because there is no proviso for altering the rule, is unable to overcome some obviously unintended yet serious difficulties, and it seems that the only way to overcome these difficulties is to adopt a developmental approach like that of legal ethics.

Utilitarianism advises that we ought to act so as to produce the greatest good for the greatest number. For those utilitarians who identify good with pleasure and bad with pain, an assessment of the morally correct action amounts to a calculation of which of the alternatives yields the highest ratio of pleasure over pain. But, as one of the classic criticisms of utilitarianism has it, just look what happens when we find we can justify as morally correct the most wicked of actions simply because it produces the greatest good for the greatest number. Consider the following example in which utilitarianism ultimately allows us to punish an innocent person in an attempt to quell widespread fear and panic among citizens of a community. This community has been terrorized recently by a mass murderer who, as yet, has not been apprehended by the police. The police have good reason to believe, from communications they have had with a person claiming to be the murderer, that this person plans to relocate permanently in a distant country. Although the murders have temporarily abated, the angry and fearful members of the public are becoming suspicious of one another, with some violence resulting from their attempts to protect themselves from others they suspect of being the mass murderer. Under these circumstances, could not the chief of police justify seizing some innocent person in the community, someone with no family ties, someone who has contributed little and for whom few care, and, with some evidence expertly fabricated, charge this person with murder and bring this person swiftly to justice? Would not the pleasure of the community far outweigh the pain inflicted on this innocent person? And have we not thus justified as correct with utilitarianism an act that clearly is morally wrong?

Now, we could, as later utilitarians did, develop a strain of utilitarianism that overcomes this difficulty. We could require that we always consider the good and bad that comes from the *practice* of acting in a certain way, here of the practice of punishing innocent people. Thinking in terms of practices, we would recognize in a moment that institutionalizing the punishment of the innocent would have little chance to contribute to the general happiness or to create more good than bad. So, on this line of reasoning, since the practice is not justifiable, the particular action is unjustifiable. This may overcome the problem with utilitarianism that we identified above, but it does so by revising the original theory, this time telling us that we are to consider the good and bad consequences not of acts but of practices. The original theory of utilitarianism that had us consider the good consequences of acts did not incorporate a proviso to the effect that we may alter how we determine moral correctness if the original theory proves to be faulty; the very nature of these systems with a single ethical standard is that they purport to have once and for all discovered the single ethical standard for the determination of ethical correctness. Such systems have to deal with exceptions in an ad hoc manner because the system has no framework for accommodating them. Herein is what I find objectionable and is why the procedure of legal ethics that provides for and requires reevaluation is both preferable and inevitable.

Turning from utilitarianism to Kantianism, we can here too see how standard criticisms of the theory are tied to a commitment to an unalterable ethical standard. Kant, of course, advised that we act only according to rules that we would be willing for everyone else to follow. But consider what happens if some fanatic were willing for everyone to follow a rule that seems clearly immoral, like "Place poison in the food of your lawyer." How could we say that the fanatic has done anything wrong when he or she acts on this rule? Has not the fanatic conformed perfectly to the dictates of Kant's moral rule? Here, as with utilitarianism, it seems we have no liberty to revise the basic moral rule to avoid clearly unintended consequences in the practical application of the rule.

In trying to correct this problem that the Kantian standard encounters, C. I. Lewis begins by identifying Kantianism's failure to take into account good and bad consequences of actions in its zeal to erect consistency of action as the hallmark of moral rectitude. Seeing himself primarily as a Kantian, he nonetheless weds with his theory some aspects of utilitarianism to overcome the deficiencies with Kant's theory. But, again, any move of this sort, laudable as it may be to preserve the spirit of the Kantian doctrine, in effect, creates for us a different ethical theory. Kant's ethics, like utilitarianism, issues us no permit to adjust its moral rule in the face of difficulties we encounter in its practical application. While we may witness utilitarian and Kantian theories needing revisions and evolving as weaknesses are perceived and as attempts are made to answer them, it must be recognized that the theories themselves do not allow this, and each time a variant is introduced to overcome difficulties, we simply have more evidence that an ethical theory or system that purports to offer a single and fixed ethical standard is an unrealistic project. In the light of this, the emerging nature of legal ethics that we identified as part of the essence of legal ethics does seem to be a desirable quality for ethics generally.

Other ethical systems, like some religious ethics, claim to have within their domain invariable rules yet seem tacitly to use the developmental approach of legal ethics. Even if there is some written formulation of these rules, as with the Ten Commandments, what will always elude human agents in their application of them will be what the lawgiver intended. When they take it upon themselves to determine that intent, these agents end up in a seemingly ludicrous position. For, on the one hand, they deny themselves the authority to make determinations of what the correct moral rules are; yet on the other, they grant themselves that authority in applying the basic rules to hard cases. Hence, they inevitably get involved in the very rule-making activity they claim to avoid.

For example, suppose there is a basic command that one ought not to kill and that this command, because it was issued by a divine creator, is not open to question or debate. Now suppose that people who accept this rule are also willing to sentence a murderer to death, to abort a fetus, to wage war, to engage in acts of self-defense. To preserve consistency, such people would claim that, although we are generally forbidden to kill, there are obvious exceptions, among them being those just cited. But as soon as exceptions are introduced, rule-making has been engaged in, in that the rule now reads that one is not to kill except to punish someone, etc. And this rule-making activity is the very one that the adherent of the religious ethics denied having the authority to undertake. If, at this point, the adherents of religious ethics invoke the intent or will of the divine commander, then it remains to be shown how they have access to this information. On the other hand, if another group of people declines to admit exceptions to the initial rule against killing, claiming that the rule admits of no explicit exceptions, these people too seem to be engaging in the activity of rule-making because they are willing to assert that the rule that forbids killing must be read as admitting of no exceptions or must be seen as having an additional clause, "and no exceptions." So, in either case, we can say that adherents end up participating in an activity much like the emerging character of legal ethics, the activity of rethinking and designing moral rules, which they claimed was for the creator alone.

Another deficiency I think fair to attribute to most ethical theories and certainly to those mentioned above is that they seem far too little concerned with the sort of person we as moral agents are. It is worth noting at this point that the orientation of legal ethics to engage in ongoing inquiries into the nature of an attorney and to tie the ethical rules governing the attorney to this conception seems to be immune from this sort of criticism, at least as far as its relevance for legal ethics goes; what sort of agents we are as attorneys is addressed head-on. Getting on with the consequences of the criticism for general ethics, I think it is fair, first off, to observe that most people wish to become moral agents but would be quite unsure how most ethical theories bear on this project, since the theories offer people little guidance in how to construct cogent conceptions of themselves as moral agents. We are not given, for example, any clear idea of what the moral agent qua utilitarian or Kantian is like as a person other than the fact that he or she is a good calculator of good and ill consequences of acts, on the one hand, or a duty-bound, consistent person, on the other. I think that what we want from a moral theory is more about the type of person we will be if we subscribe to the view. People are very much concerned about what the activity compelled by some moral theory says about them as persons. Utilitarianism, on that count, is objectionable in some forms not simply because of the theoretical imperfection of its possibly compelling the act we perceive to be immoral, as noted above, but, more important, because this theory compels us in that instance to be the sort of person we would not want to be. And the Kantian directive of setting aside all inclination—even the desire to do good—and act out of a sense of duty for the universalizable maxim portrays an aspect of personality that would be perceived by most, I would guess, as overly rigid and hardly the sort of quality most would want to define them as persons.

In accord with this line of reasoning that rejects the models of the moral agent that traditional theory offers are Carol Gilligan and Owen Flanagan. Gilligan argues that considerations of justice, rights, obligations, and duties are all part of the male's way of thinking about morality. She opts for an ethics of care tied to the female way, which emphasizes caring attitudes and actions and the development of interpersonal relations as the stuff of moral reality.[58] Flanagan wants to break moral thinking from the stronghold of the single rule–oriented ethics of Kantianism and utilitarianism. While sympathetic with Gilligan's attempt to carve out an alternative, Flanagan dismisses her tying approaches to morality to male and female ways of thinking. In addition, Flanagan rejects Gilligan's depicting only two main alternatives for thinking about moral personality. Flanagan urges that we think of moral personality as "a more variegated and heterogeneous sort of thing than is typically thought."[59] He sees moral personality as resulting from a creative process and ties this insight to the thinking of his favorite philosopher, William James, the American pragmatist. Flanagan's view is similar to mine, as becomes evident in the next section, where I explore the pragmatic elements of the procedure of legal ethics. But what also becomes evident is that neither Flanagan's approach nor any general pragmatic approach establishes the intimate connection between the conceptions we construct of ourselves and rules for conduct.

THE PRAGMATIC FEATURES OF LEGAL ETHICS

If the features of legal ethics seem desirable for an ethical theory in that they allow us to overcome some of the difficulties associated with some major moves in general ethics, what might we say about the philosophical character of these features? The answer to this question helps us to determine further the character of legal ethics and to make explicit how what we learn from it might be incorporated into general ethics and used to enrich the further development of legal ethics. I think it fair to observe that what we have said about legal ethics makes it philosophically pragmatic in some *prima facie* fashion. I am here drawing attention to the distinctively American contribution to philosophy—pragmatism—that urges us to turn from faulty, fixed, or static conceptions of ourselves and our world to those which are useful and true because of their utility.

Much influenced by Darwin's thesis about the emergence of life forms, early pragmatists like Chauncey Wright, Charles Sanders Peirce, William James, and John Dewey constructed the analog of evolving organisms for such notions as truth and knowledge, indicating their developing nature and inveighing against any Platonic understanding of truth as being fixed, absolute, and awaiting our discovery as such. Continuing in this vein, contemporary pragmatists like Scheffler, Goodman, Lewis, and Quine have effected similar revisions in the manner in which we deal with our system of beliefs. They draw our attention to the insight that no belief, even what we consider a law of logic, is beyond alteration in the name of pragmatic advance, that even such dearly held beliefs should be seen as nothing more than a useful means by which people have ordered their world to make it intelligible and their lives in it productive.

With this said, in what ways might we say that some ethical theory is pragmatic? Some major alternatives are as follows:

1. an ethical theory that is developed as an analog to some well-developed pragmatic approach in some other area of philosophy, say, epistemology;

2. an ethical theory that bears pragmatic characteristics;

3. an ethical theory that is nothing more than pragmatism itself, a single theory or orientation or philosophy that alone suffices to resolve any issue that may have been considered peculiarly ethical and in need of a special theory;

4. the ethical theory that works best; and

5. a practical ethical theory.

Our goal in exploring these possibilities will be a sense of what pragmatic ethical theories have in common. This comparison should shed light not just on the nature of pragmatic ethical theories but on that of legal ethics, too, which we found to bear initial similarities to pragmatic ethics. Other writers, it might be noted, have remarked on the varying ways in which pragmatism might be conceived. In a well-known essay, "The Thirteen Pragmatisms,"[60] Arthur Lovejoy merely lists the varying conceptions of pragmatism, leaving the reader with the overall impression that some pejorative comment is being made about this unfortunate philosophy whose essence can be formulated in, of all things, thirteen ways. Our attempt is a more sympathetic one, in that we strive to factor out of the diversity some uniformity and indeed observe eventually that this diversity teaches us that *there is no single touchstone of truth in ethics and that, as we have observed about legal ethics, a pragmatic ethics seems to embrace a developmental approach about how best to deal with ethical problems.*

Let us turn to the first of the possibilities mentioned above. This form of pragmatic ethics can best be illustrated by considering how some pragmatists have dealt with systems of beliefs. Consider such holistic pragmatists as Goodman, Scheffler, and Quine. Scheffler's model, for example, organizes our beliefs in the empirical sciences into a system and provides principles for the acceptance of new beliefs and the rejection of old. The model is a thoroughgoing pragmatic model in that anything in our system of beliefs, from a report of what I am presently perceiving to a law of logic, can be rejected if it challenges the overall credibility of the system. Among

Scheffler's principles to justify this is: "We justify the acceptance of A at time t by showing that its total credible value at t is not less than that of any of its contemporary rivals."[61] Again, we know what is of primary significance for a viable system of beliefs—overall credibility—and we make changes where necessary; we allow the system to develop, in the name of furthering credibility.

The model, if adapted to the instant problem of dealing with a system of moral rules, would have us substitute rules for beliefs and revise the acceptance principle to one appropriate for rules rather than beliefs. Ability to elicit willing conformity may be the characteristic virtue of a system of rules and may be the analog of credibility, the characteristic virtue of a system of beliefs. I say this because credibility is not chiefly at issue with rules as it is with a system of beliefs. While we may say that we believe in the teachings of various moral or legal principles—"I believe it is wrong to kill," "I believe in affirmative action for minorities"—such attitudes of belief are irrelevant to the efficacy of such rules in a society if its citizens or moral agents are unwilling to conform to the rules. Further, one of the purposes of such a system is to direct behavior to the achievement of certain ends. Unless the rules are followed, the use of some system to effect a given end is futile. Accordingly, a willingness to conform seems fundamental. If so, we can say that we justify acceptance of one moral system over its contemporary rivals if, other things being equal, it elicits a greater willingness to conform, and we justify accepting a particular rule or directive into a particular system if, other things being equal, it becomes part of the system to which we are most willing to conform. So, if we think of a system of moral rules as analogous to how some pragmatists have thought of a system of beliefs, we would be willing to allow the moral system to change and develop in the name of achieving what seems to be the primary purpose of the system. And this would be the case regardless of how we conceived of the primary purpose or the chief virtue.

C. I. Lewis's ethics, I think, is representative of a theory that bears pragmatic characteristics, and thus of option 2 stated previously. It is not a thoroughgoing pragmatic ethics, given the presence of strong Kantian motifs, like an unchanging categorical imperative rooted in our apprehension of human nature, but the fashion in which Lewis overcomes some of the problems associated with the Kantian imperative noted above is indicative of the pragmatist's dislike for fixity. This flexibility of Lewis's ethics is accomplished, in part, by his employment of a theory of value that has us learn of values through our interaction with the world and that shows values to play an important role in our determining moral right and wrong. Echoed here are some clear pragmatic commitments to the interrelations between knowledge and action, not to mention the pragmatist's familiar goal of breaking down any sharp division between facts and values. Says Lewis, "Knowledge, action, and evaluation are essentially connected. The primary and pervasive significance of knowledge lies in its guidance of action: knowing is for the sake of doing. And action, obviously, is rooted in evaluation."[62]

Lewis calls his moral rule "The Principle of Equality Before the Moral Law"; it is the counterpart in Lewis's ethics to Kant's moral rule urging consistency in action, and it advises that "we take no decision of action which is a member of any class of decisions of doing all members of which you would call upon others to avoid."[63] According to Lewis, this rule indeed requires consistency of action, but, unlike Kant's rule, it has other requirements. Besides the "formal and explicit" criteria, there are "contextual and implicit" criteria in the moral law. They involve "what is implicit in reference to 'you'" and turn on two factors: (1) "that acts are to be judged according to their good or bad consequences,"[64] and (2) "that such good or evil of their effects is to be assessed from the viewpoint of those upon whom these effects are visited."[65] This formulation invites an introduction into our reasoning about the moral correctness of an action a consideration of good and bad consequences of the act. Such considerations, on Lewis's analysis, are empirical considerations that can be determined on a footing similar to any determinations of fact in the empirical sciences. And just as our determinations of fact in the sciences bear the distinctive qualities of being based on, and testable in, experience and being subject to revision and development as experience advises, such is exactly the case with our objective claims of value, claims of what is objectively good and bad. So, essentially wedded to Lewis's Kantian vision of there being a correct ethical standard is a component that requires our taking into account our emerging understanding of what is good and bad in human experience.

Remarks Dewey has made about ethics seem to place him most squarely within ethical theory (3) in that he seems committed to the pragmatic approach being no different in the area of ethics than it is in any other area of human endeavor. For example, Dewey brings out that we must turn from simplistic models of ethics where we see our moral experience as being little more than applying moral rules, like "Don't cheat," to clear-cut situations, like one in which one fabricates evidence for presentation at trial. We should recognize that complex issues or problems arise in our moral experience just as in any other area of human endeavor. And as with any area, it is thought that is turned to for the solution of the problem; it is as we find some solution to be effective in dealing with certain problems that we begin to formulate principles and generalizations and use these as guides when similar problems occur: again, whether in science, morals, or elsewhere in human experience. We may attach weight to these principles, and do so justifiably if they have endured, but that gives them no special status as being permanently authoritative. Moral principles, Dewey tells us, "are no more to be lightly discarded than are scientific principles worked out in the past. But in one as in the other, newly discovered facts or newly instituted conditions may give rise to doubts and indicate the inapplicability of accepted doctrines."[66]

Ethical theory 4 from the list focuses our attention on that aspect of the pragmatic creed concerning the interrelation between correctness and what works. James, for example, rejects those conceptions of truth that portray it as "an inert static relation,"[67] where, once we have determined that there is agreement between the belief and its object, we claim that we have arrived at the truth and remain at a resting state: "When you've got your true idea of anything, there's an end of the matter. You're in possession; you *know*; you have fulfilled your destiny.... Epistemologically you are in stable equilibrium."[68] Interested in tying the truth of an idea to its practical significance, James defines true ideas as *"those that we can assimilate, validate, corroborate and verify....* The truth of an idea is not a stagnant property inherent in it. Truth *happens* to an idea. It *becomes* true, is made true by events. Its verity *is* in fact an event, a process: the process namely of its verifying itself, its *verification*. Its validity is the process of its *validation*."[69] James introduces his conception of truth as "what works" as he turns to his discussion of theories and our choice among competing theories: "We must find a theory that will *work*; for our theory must mediate between all previous truths and certain new experiences. It must derange common sense and previous belief as little as possible, and it must lead to some sensible terminus or other that can be verified exactly."[70] It seems that in applying this view to ethical theories, we could select as best for human use any of those mentioned above—Kantian, utilitarian, customary—so long as they work. The interesting thing that emerges from this selection is that, regardless of the extent to which any of these theories bear the markings of pragmatism, in the present sense of "pragmatic," we can see them as pragmatic ethical theories so long as they have been delivered up as correct by the pragmatic notion of correctness.

Ethical theory 5 makes us mindful that we need not, when using the word *pragmatic,* be referring to, or invoking, a tradition in philosophy, but only suggesting the practical in general. For our purposes of finding the significance of pragmatism for ethical theory, we might recognize that *practical* suggests for ethics its ability to offer specific pieces of advice for everyday moral problems, its allowing one to bend from fixed principles, its allowing one to set these principles aside because of the exigencies of some situation, or its offering common-sense solutions to problems. So, ethical theory 5, with its practical bent, is no more committed to rigid application of fixed and unchanging moral rules to moral problems than the other theories. By depicting moral systems as changing to further the system's chief virtue, by incorporating an emerging understanding of good and bad, by underscoring how accepted doctrine is always subject to change, or by describing truth as a process for achieving what works, the other theories fall in line with ethical theory 5.

As noted above, one thing that becomes evident from this survey is that virtually all pragmatic approaches have in common some notion that ethical problems may be solved in various fashions without nagging doubt that we have overlooked *the truth* about the matter. Any disquiet about a moral theory's having this quality seems to be a function of an insistence on there being a single answer or solution to any question or problem as suggested by some mathematical model of inquiry. But that obviously is not the only model we have to work with in the area of inquiry. We are all aware, for example, that in the area of medicine, one can draw on a number of fields in dealing with a single problem. Consider the treatment of an ulcer. Surgery is possible; the use of medication is possible; psychiatric treatment is possible. We do not insist that the medical community decide, once and for all, what the one method will be. Moreover, we recognize that each of these approaches has deficiencies and strengths, yet we turn to them as basically reliable, each being an effective way of dealing with the problem as against, say, administering a lethal dose of potassium cyanide to the patient, incinerating the patient, or pulling the patient's hair out by its roots.

Further, we are familiar with how, in law, the problem of how one's estate will be settled, for example, is hardly a function of taking some simple and true principle of probate law, applying it to the facts of the case, and obtaining the correct settlement. We know that we may be turning to principles and rules from the body of tax regulations as we may find applicable various rules and principles from tort, contract, and property law. Here we draw on varying domains of the law, each with its own justifying principles and each with its own purposes; we know, for example, that the basic, underlying principles of contract law are geared toward insuring freedom of contracting among willing, self-interested, rational agents for their mutual benefit, whereas in tort law, the idea is to allow means for redressing unwanted interferences with one's self or property. How these rules from these varying areas of the law will influence the settlement of the estate will be a function of, to name a couple of significant factors, what the testator wished to achieve, along with the interests of the beneficiaries. Thus, suppose that the testator devises a life estate to his first son in the family ranch; the ranch is currently occupied by the testator's second son, who says he will not surrender possession. The first son, feeling that his having already received the testator's coastal property is enough, does not wish to interfere with his brother's current enjoyment of the ranch. Obviously the executor could bring a suit for ejectment of the first brother from the ranch, although, in the interest of constructing a viable settlement, the measure would hardly seem indicated.

Another way of looking at the claim here is that the pragmatic moral theorist and agent are much like one who is engaged in some area of purposive human action and is trying to create or build in accord with various goals and interests. Consider how the technologist proceeds, attempting to create in the world what seems to further our condition, be it artificial limbs, speeding jets, or nuclear reactors. It would seem odd indeed if we were to ask whether the creations of these technologists are true of the world. Rather, we measure the technologists' success in terms of the worthiness of their goals and the extent to which their actions and the fruits thereof allow the goals to be realized. Here, as with our other examples from medicine and law, we recognize that some mathematical model of problem-solving that delivers up a single right answer simply does not apply.

Now, if this consideration of the essence of a pragmatic ethical theory assists us with our understanding of what the distinctive and positive qualities of legal ethics are, it is because it makes explicit and more evident aspects of what we first observed. We found it to be the case that legal ethics requires lawyers to participate in an ongoing and critical assessment of just how the attorney is to be conceived and in devising rules of conduct that follow from and fit this conception. We saw how this approach gives legal ethics an advantage over other ethical theories and in what sense it can serve as a model for general ethics. We considered how the possibility of using legal ethics as a model would forever be obscured were we to think in the terms set by the traditional debate. That debate, we saw, narrowly presented two main possibilities—that legal ethics is or should be subsumed by general ethics or that legel ethics is essentially different from general ethics.

We deepened our understanding of the positive qualities of legal ethics that could serve as a model for general ethics by investigating pragmatic ethical theory. We now recognize that the project is not one of discovering some eternal wisdom about the absolute obligations of the attorney, no more so than with any pragmatic ethical theory. Further, we are able now to recognize that there may well be some viable alternatives for conceiving of the attorney just as we saw that with any pragmatic approach in ethics, plausible alternative answers and solutions may well be available to various questions and problems. While all of the pragmatic theories were consistent with the emerging nature of legal ethics, none clearly captured the connection we observed in legal ethics between the conceptions of roles that emerged and the rules to guide conduct. Further, we are looking for a theory that captures all of the desirable qualities of legal ethics and that is general enough to apply to anyone if we are to make good on an insistence that general ethics be like legal ethics. It is to the development of this theory that we will turn in the next chapter.

KLEE, Paul. *Six Species*. 1930. Watercolor on cotton cloth, 11-1/2 x18-3/4". Collection, Flex Klee, Bern.

2

Human Nature

In chapter 1 we observed how legal ethics displayed pragmatic features desirable for ethical theory insofar as it embraced a commitment to developing a conception of the lawyer and to bringing that to bear on the lawyer's conduct in the form of rules that are derived from the conception. Here we will explore more fully what it means to draw on legal ethics as a model for general ethics. We investigate the feasibility of developing conceptions of our various roles, thinking even of human nature as open for construction, and of tying rules of conduct to these conceptions. In so doing, we will develop a theory of human nature that grounds not just the lawyer's ethics, but anyone's.

The theory, simply put, is this. Our nature allows us to construct, in an ongoing process, conceptions of ourselves ranging from our specific roles to our humanity itself, with these conceptions suggesting guidelines for our conduct. Suppose, for example, that our thinking about ourselves as humans leads us to conceive of ourselves as rational beings, as competitive but social and striving to progress. Going hand in hand with this construction are such evident guidelines and admonitions for conduct as to act with forethought, to act rationally, to compete, and to progress. The constructed concept in effect is a normative one and as such brings with it rules to govern our experience. Further, I bring out how we develop these conceptions and follow their advice in a social context where role modeling is a reality and where it makes sense to recognize a duty to act only in ways that we are willing for others to imitate. This ethical component is evidently closely tied to our theory of human nature, and we will explore the dimensions of this component in the concluding chapter. Here we focus on elaborating on and establishing our view of human nature.

Highlighting this view's distinctive ideas that humans can develop an understanding of themselves and that tied to this understanding are guidelines for conduct, we can refer to human persons summarily as *constructors of rule-referring conceptions of themselves*. In what follows, I draw no sharp distinction between constructing a view of one's nature as a human being and a view of oneself as a human self, and I use the two interchangeably, for as soon as the self is described as a human self, we are already requiring of the description a generality that would include all humans and thus would apply to human nature. Also, I am conceiving of us broadly here to include our human condition, our roles and even our environments insofar as they are extensions of our identities.

Our discussion of this view of humans as ethical self-constructors will take us first to an exploration of how the strategy of investigating the interrelations of human nature and ethics, as well as the particular view itself, is suggested, in part, by a number of Western moral theories. Next, in arguing for the cogency of the view, I present a variety of cognate views, both to lend support to this type of endeavor and to distinguish my view from these related efforts. I then turn to further considerations and arguments to refine the view and to incline the reader to recognize its merits. I conclude with a discussion of the practical significance of this view of human nature for enriching our thinking about legal ethics.

WAYS IN WHICH A STUDY OF ETHICAL THEORY SUGGESTS
BOTH A METHODOLOGY AND A FIRST APPROXIMATION
OF THE VIEW

That there is a connection between how we see ourselves and what
we ought to be doing is neither novel nor, upon reflection, particularly surprising. Says one commentator:

> Different views about human nature lead naturally to different
> conclusions about what we ought to do and how we can do it. If
> God made us, then it is His purpose that defines what we ought
> to be, and we must look to him for help. If we are made by our
> society, and if we find that our life is somehow unsatisfactory,
> then there can be no real cure until society is transformed.[1]

Surely investigating human nature in an effort to determine what
our obligations are has initial plausibility in that it makes little sense
to demand of people that they act in some way that they are unable
to, or, more specifically for our purposes, that they ought morally to
do something that their nature precludes them from doing.

In what follows, we observe that a recurring methodology in
Western ethics for determining our moral obligations has us look first
to human nature. Our look at the theories of the ethical egoist's,
Plato's, Bentham's, and Epictetus's proves useful for our project
since, for one thing, it provides the context within which we are operating when we ground our obligations in our nature as we do here.
For another, and more important, the survey itself lends support to
the view we are developing. We find that each account of human
nature and its related ethical advice seems plausible. Since we can see
ourselves and our guidelines for conduct in various ways, it makes
sense to ask how we can best conceive of ourselves and to derive our
guidelines for conduct from the conception which we construct.

Let us begin with ethical egoism. Psychological egoism, a theory of human nature, has been used to argue for ethical egoism, the
ethical theory. Psychological egoism basically asserts that essential to

understanding human motivation is a consideration of self-interest, that humans are unable to act unless they think the action will further their own good, well being or interest. Accepting the truth of the psychological egoist's description of human nature, one can argue for the obligatory claim that one always ought to act so as to further one's own good, well being or interest. The argument proceeds by bringing out first a necessary condition for having an obligation— that one has an obligation to do something only if one is able to do it. At this point in the argument, the thesis of psychological egoism is introduced, pointing out that one is psychologically able to do something only if one thinks it furthers one's own good, well being, or interest. From these considerations we can conclude that one has an obligation to do something only if one thinks it furthers one's own good, well being or interest. Put differently, this line of reasoning shows how a statement of our self-interested nature, coupled simply with a claim about the nature of any obligation, requires a view that self-interest is the crux of our ethical obligations. In short, we ought to do what we are naturally motivated to do—to further self interest.

Some theorists show that an ethical norm is required of us upon our accepting a certain enriched account of human nature as accurate.[2] Let us consider as an example Plato's analysis of human nature wherein the human soul is divided into three faculties—reason, the spirited element, and the desires or appetites. In Plato's account, any one of these three faculties may overpower the other two. We may have, for example, a soul bent on satisfying one or more desires, setting reason aside as it does so. To be sure, pleasures are attendant upon the satisfaction of these desires. But the consequence is twofold. First, one misses out on the best and truest pleasures that accompany the pursuits of reason, and, second, one whose reason does not control the soul fails to lead the just life. So, to the extent we wish to assert what one ought to do to be just, namely, that one ought to allow reason to control the soul, we must make reference to human nature, the three elements of the soul, and the role of reason in keeping the soul in good working order.

Bentham proffers an account of human nature known as psychological hedonism according to which the explanation of human motivation hinges on our inability to act otherwise than to pursue pleasure and avoid pain. Bentham's utilitarian credo of acting so as to produce the greatest good for the greatest number in effect requires us to produce the greatest pleasure for the greatest number, since Bentham equates good with pleasure. The famous first sentence of his work, *The Principles of Morals and Legislation,* shows him unmistakably to be connecting what we ought to do with our nature: "Nature has placed mankind under the governance of two sovereign masters, *pain* and *pleasure.* It is for them alone to point out what we ought to do, as well as to determine what we shall do."[3]

Let us look at the thinking of the ancient Stoic philosopher, Epictetus, for one further illustration of one's grounding one's ethical advice in a theory of human nature. On Epictetus's account of our nature, some things, like choice and desire, are within our control; others, like property and reputation, are not, and his basic advice is to avoid that which is not. As Epictetus's philosophy unfolds, it becomes clear that we are to pursue only that which is within our control; the consequences of doing so include the avoidance of harm that comes from dabbling in affairs beyond our control, and happiness, a happiness that results from our developing a calm, steadfast attitude toward the world, an attitude of *apatheia.*

Having considered examples of ethical theories variously indebted to conceptions of human nature, we are prepared to make some general observations and to show how they bear on the theory we are establishing. One thing is certain, of course. Not all of these views can be correct, since each is inconsistent with the other. That one ought to look out for oneself is, quite simply, a command of a different sort than one that obligates us to look out for the greatest number. It is fruitful, however, to follow up on what these theories seem to be in agreement on, namely, that there is a close connection between our nature as humans and what is morally incumbent upon us. First, I find that all the foregoing characterizations of human nature, and others not examined here, do have some ring of truth and, in my experience teaching these theories, have similar rings of truth for my students. We view ourselves quite differently at different times, and, under those circumstances, the corresponding moral guidelines that ethicists have suggested not only seem sensible but also appropriate and natural to introduce against the backdrop of a particular description of human nature. From our willingness to embrace such diverging descriptions of ourselves, I gather something quite constant in human nature—that humans are creatures capable of perceiving themselves in variable fashions and that they naturally construct guidelines for their conduct based on these perceptions.

Let us persist in this free associating for a moment longer to complete a first approximation of the idea. That one tends to construct guidelines for one's actions based on one's perception of oneself does not suggest that just any perception or guideline is justifiable or desirable. As will become clearer in the concluding chapter, we construct these conceptions and guidelines in a social context, in which it is reasonable to expect that others may imitate our behavior. An important restraint then on the view and guidelines that we adopt is that we be willing for others to act likewise. Further, given this view of our malleable nature, it seems that we can sensibly ask what would be worthwhile fashions for humans to see themselves; it is this line of reasoning that allows us to introduce the notion of one's constructing a conception. From there we can proceed to inquire about the norms suggested for a human so conceived. And on like reasoning, we can ask similar questions for the human in various roles and environments.

So, this brief survey of ethical theory and how it draws on a theory of human nature has been instructive on two important counts. First, it provides illustrations of a recurring strategy in ethical theory, which helps to make clear the purpose of the strategy. Again, an important motivation for considering human nature in the context of searching for ethical advice is to ensure that the agent is capable of acting in accord with the ethical prescription. The claim that it is natural for humans, or that it is part of human nature, to perceive the rules making claims on their activity as being relative to their conception of themselves reflects, in part, our awareness of the dependence of an obligation on an ability.

Second, and more important, in trying to make sense of the existence of the multiplicity of plausible accounts of human nature, we were led to realize that our view both accounts for the phenomena and follows inductively from the data. More concretely, the basic form of this argument would be as follows:

1. Ethical theorist$_A$ portrays human nature as A, and, based on that, argues how ethically we ought to act, all of which seems plausible.
2. Ethical theorist$_B$ portrays human nature as B, and, based on that, argues how ethically we ought to act, all of which seems plausible....
3. Ethical theorist$_N$ portrays human nature as N, and, based on that, argues how ethically we ought to act, all of which seems plausible.

Thus,

4. We find that we can and do see our nature in a variety of plausible ways, each of which provides a basis for constructing guidelines for conduct.

Thus,

5. It makes sense for us to construct a fruitful view of our nature from which we can reasonably determine guidelines for our conduct.

Before moving on to develop further support for our view, let us make it clear that no universal generalization is being made about there being some invariable connection between one's theorizing about human nature and one's offering ethical advice. Some theories of human nature leave open the question of what we ought to be doing morally, and it is fairly clear that their formulation was not with the intent to answer questions about our moral obligations. For example, in identifying our nature, one theorist draws our attention to an anatomical criterion as well as a psychological one involving the ability to make and execute decisions.[4] Another constructs a synthesis of various conceptions of our nature, suggesting that we are, at once, a natural, cultural/communal, intellectual, and existential being with no follow-up on our obligations.[5] An emphasis on the interrelatedness of our nature with technology also is silent on morality.[6] Somewhat in sympathy with my point here is a commentator who claims to *narrow* his subject matter to the relevance of human nature to morality.[7] His doing so draws on the observation that much can be said about human nature that is irrelevant to morality, whereas, as I have been urging, there is good reason in constructing a moral theory to inquire into various views about our nature, recognizing that some of these are indeed relevant.

COGNATE VIEWS

With that qualification, let us continue with a development of our view of human nature, for which we have adduced some inductive support from the legacy of Western ethics. At this point, I think it is worth noting that some theorists, in commenting on the views of human nature of others or in developing their own views of human nature, have mentioned the plausibility of a view similar to the one we are developing. In attempting to reconcile externalism, where morality is seen as alien to human nature, with internalism, where morality is inherent in human nature, Cua brings out that the question of human nature is a question we pose to ourselves; he portrays the human as the self-defining, self-interpreting animal. His view, he says, is quasi-pragmatic in that he treats different views of human nature as suggestions for understanding the human predicament.[8] In assessing the parameters of the debate over the selfish-gene theory, Thompson first surveys Dawkins's contention concerning the primacy of self-interest, Kropotkin's claim that, while we are self-interested, we are equally social, and Singer's attempt to put the selfish-gene theory in perspective by dubbing it a reality but assigning to reason primacy over biology. Thompson concludes that human nature may be less fixed than we have thought and points to the significance of how humans view themselves.[9]

But the language of such authors is tentative, and their insights are left unanalyzed. Cua, for example, says, "Perhaps, in the end, it is his own interpretation of his humanity that counts as his essence."[10] And Thompson employs a mode of "it seems that" "it is possible that" to express this observation: "It would seem that any ethic, any political philosophy, which centers on the self-fulfillment and happiness of human individuals should, if at all possible, leave room for the expression of characteristics which are fundamental to the way human beings view themselves.... If what we take to be human nature depends on our point of view—on what we regard as essential to our lives—then it is possible that this nature may turn out to be less fixed than we have supposed."[11] Again, the point is that others have had insights friendly to ours, but the thinking aimed at establishing these insights is relatively undeveloped.

Other, similar views, while perhaps more fully worked out than the foregoing, diverge in important ways from ours. Milton Fisk, for example, brings out that human nature can change but ties this capacity for change strictly to social context and does so for the purpose ultimately of arguing that socialism is compatible with human communities: "To sum up: There is no impossibility about adjusting human nature to socialism. The fundamental reason for this is that human nature is not something that is inherent in people but is something that derives in some important ways from the social context in which they live. In particular it derives from the class, the race, the sex to which they belong. Thus human nature can change as groups change."[12] Mead, too, is classically associated with a view that the self develops through a social process and that our nature is not fixed at birth; it "develops in a given individual as a result of his relationships to that process as a whole and to other individuals within that process."[13] But Mead's view, like Fisk's, while similar to ours and less sketchy than some of the notions above, still is essentially committed to accounting for the development of self as part of a social process that seems to happen to the individual rather than as a result of the reflective, constructive process characteristic of our view. Nonetheless, it is relevant in establishing our view that others who have worked with the teachings of Western ethics have offered speculations on what it ultimately suggests about our nature and that these speculations bear close resemblances to ours.

FURTHER DEVELOPMENT AND REFINEMENT OF THE VIEW: THE CONSTRUCTION AND ITS CONNECTION WITH RULES

Let us now turn to exploring further two significant aspects of our view of humans as constructors of rule-referring conceptions of their nature, namely, the tenet concerning the construction (and its relationship to rules) and that concerning our rule-guided nature. First, let us look more closely at the construction itself and, in particular, at the relevance of the claim, and its supporting evidence, that we can and do see ourselves in different fashions. Consider, to begin with, just a few pieces of such evidence. As mentioned above, I can offer testimony that as we move from one theory of human nature to another in an ethics class, students do find much plausibility in each; students report that each theory throws new light on how they see themselves. Further, one can turn to anthropological and historical data that point to variability in human nature. Fromm and Xirau observe that "an examination of the history of humanity suggests that man in our epoch is so different from man in previous ones that it is unrealistic to assume that men in every historical epoch have had in common that essence which can be called 'human nature'";[14] they go on to bring out that "the study of the so-called primitive peoples has shown such a diversity of customs, values, feelings, and thoughts that many anthropologists arrived at the concept that man is born as a blank sheet of paper on which each culture writes its text."[15]

For more support for our claim about humans seeing their nature in different ways, consider the varying conceptions of human nature promulgated by world religions and the fact that peoples of the world see themselves in these differing ways. Hinduism, with its caste system, shows there to be inherent inequalities among humans, with privileges attaching to members of the upper classes that are denied to the laborers, the lowest class; a priest, a woman, or a merchant is permitted to acquire knowledge of the Veda, the sacred scriptures, access to which is forbidden the laborer. Jainism depicts people as being partly soul, partly matter. The omniscient and blissful nature of the soul is obscured through its association with matter and through the operation of a force, Karma. The Jain's goal is to eliminate Karmic matter. In the Buddhist view, the human is a series of transitory mental and physical states; there is no enduring or eternal self. Further, a human is a being who suffers but who can attain a state of peace and insight, nirvana, by conforming to various requirements for ethical conduct and mental training set out in the Noble Eightfold Path. In the Christian view, humans, as sinful creatures, are offered forgiveness by God through his son, Jesus Christ. Further, humans can, through their faith in Christ, achieve a state of full consciousness of God's presence, as they enter heaven at death.[16]

Now, the question arises as to whether a recognition that humans can and do see themselves in different ways, as suggested above, also places us in a position to construct some conception of ourselves. If we are able to see ourselves differently in accord with the varying portraits of human nature we receive and yet claim that we ourselves are not able to construct a concept of our nature, then we seem to be placing ourselves in an absurd situation; we abandon any claim of competency on our part to do so and recognize the ability only in others—surely these depictions we choose from were constructed by someone or some group of people.

Faced with this line of reasoning that attempts to make plausible the idea of our constructing a view of our nature, one may object that we are led to ignore the "true" conception of human nature. But it seems that the burden lies on those who insist on a single, fixed conception to show that our dealings with our nature are so different from theorizing about so many other areas of our experience where there exist competing and viable ways of structuring and understanding them; in such cases, it seems, the best way to explain the existence of alternative conceptions is to recognize that no single one embraces the truth. We know well and acknowledge how, in the realm of our practical experience, there are generally a number of good ways of solving a problem or effecting some outcome—more than one way of making a cake, building a house, writing a will, of leading a healthy life, of treating a disease, of hosting a party. Thus, as one selects activities conducive to health, jogging may be chosen over bicycling for good circulation, a vegetarian diet over one generally low in red meats to avoid saturated fats, cutting down on smoking and drinking or giving them up. In these areas of planned or purposive human activity, the means we adopt to accomplish the end invariably is a construction of the options available, with the possibilities for the number of constructions being a function of the combinations of decisions on the options. Again, the claim here is that we might think of our dealing with our nature as much like our dealing with many other areas of our experience where we have latitude to construct a conception that guides our actions.

More directly, we can turn to Sartre and Hesse, who provide us with a couple of good examples of how one can and does construct a concept of oneself. At the close of his novel *Nausea*, Sartre portrays how Roquentin, the protagonist, moves from his encounter with nothingness to a construction of a new self, drawing on variables ranging from his skills as a writer of history, to his interest in adventure, to his desire to share with others what he learned about human existence from his experience with nothingness. He gives his life meaning as he creates a life for himself where he is a writer of adventure stories. As this self-construction unfolds, we first find Roquentin observing, in the context of trying to justify his existence after his encounter with nothingness, that: "I am like a man completely frozen after a trek through the snow and who suddenly comes into a warm room. I think he would stay motionless near the door...."[17] Then his thoughts turn to a course of action based on the restructuring of what he was and his interest now in creating a meaningful essence upon coming to grips with his having no given essence: "Couldn't I try.... It would have to be a book: I don't know how to do anything else. But not a history book.... A story, for example, something that could never happen, an adventure. It would be beautiful and hard as steel and make people ashamed of their existence."[18]

And in *Steppenwolf*, Hesse depicts the wide range of possibilities available in the process of constructing the human self and the seemingly infinite variety of ways in which they can be manifested. At the close of this novel, Steppenwolf, the psychologically shattered main character, visits a sage who identifies himself as "not anybody"[19] and who offers Steppenwolf "instruction in the building up of the personality."[20] Steppenwolf's adviser brings out that "we demonstrate to anyone...that he can rearrange these pieces of a previous self in what order he pleases, and so attain to an endless multiplicity of moves in the game of life";[21] he identifies the process as "the act of life."[22]

Up to this point, we have considered some initial reasons for supporting the idea that we can and do see ourselves differently and that we are able to construct a concept of self. We noted how anthropological and historical data in tandem with the accounts of human nature we get from different religions point to how humans have embraced conceptions of themselves that differ radically from each other. We saw how it made sense to move from the phenomenon of humans conceiving of themselves differently to their capacity to construct a view of themselves; in part we drew on the fashion in which a construction of a view of self was analogous to how we dealt with many areas of our practical experience. And we considered some illustrations of literary characters effecting such a construction.

In further developing our view, we should note that it allows us to make sense of a variety of phenomena we commonly observe. Consider people's formulating and following a life plan, acting in accord with ideals or imitating role models, people's converting from one religion to another, or their seeking psychological counsel for a problem. All of these acts presuppose that we are able to become something that we presently are not, ranging from a change in how we see ourselves in some particular role to how we see ourselves as humans. What becomes apparent when we consider such situations as instances of self-construction is that they entail integrally related rules for future conduct. Let us investigate this further.

Consider students developing career paths where, in so doing, they may take into account what their course work has been to this point, what their options and preferences for work for the future are, and what their aptitudes and capabilities are; consider how they forge these factors into goals depicting what they want to become and how the adoption of these goals brings with it subsidiary plans or rules for behavior for achieving the end. The student selecting law as a career goal now plans to take the LSAT examination, to write to law schools for applications, to line up references, and to join the pre-law society. Consider the person who wishes to be the sympathetic judge, the persnickety teacher, the gracious grandmother, the vivacious socialite—each recognizing that, if he or she is to adopt such a personality, he or she must conform to certain patterns of activity.

Consider one who converts from one religion to another, and in so doing, rejects one view of humans and what they should be doing and adopting another. Consider a Christian who endorses a view of human nature whereby residing in the body is an incorporeal, rational soul that can ascend to heaven after the death of the body—but not live later in the body of, say, a cow. Then that person becomes a Hindu. Hindu teaching shows the soul now in the human body as capable of living later in that of a cow. This convert not only embraces a different view of human nature but agrees to observe prescriptions about the treatment of cows, like their nonuse as a source of food, that are not part of the Christian view.

Let us continue to explore how our view of human nature allows us to account for other common phenomena besides planned activity and religious conversion—here of dealing with mental instability—and how rules for conduct are related. The neurotic state of mind is sometimes characterized as one that places some idealized conception upon the world when the conception does not fit, and the consequence is the generation of distress for the organism. This description of neurosis seems to make certain assumptions about the normal mind or about human nature regarding how the human mind should operate if a person is to avoid distress and presumably be happy.

How does the nonneurotic mind confront the world? Apparently it encounters the world with a conception that does in some sense fit or square with the course of events. If we were to straighten out Madame Emma Bovary's mind, for example, we would begin by detailing in what sense she dissimulates reality with her idealized conceptions. We are told how, when she was a child studying with the nuns, she idealized various rituals, stories, and routines, taking pleasure in the perception of their beauty. We see how, later, this idealization of religious life is replaced by a lofty and pleasant conception of love in human relations. This conception of love causes Emma Bovary to detest her husband for falling short of her ideal and to flit from romance to romance in a futile search that brings her agony, humiliation, and mental breakdown. The Madame, we suspect, would be happier if she could alter her conception of what she wants from her love life, if she could favor one that allows her to be aware of the positive qualities in her relation with her husband or the possibility of creating an acceptable relationship with him, one that allows her to see how she is being or can be exploited by others whom she considers as candidates for her idealized love, one that allows for a self-awareness of how her present conception is in part the cause of her misery and boredom. In short, the nonneurotic self-conception seems to be a revised conception that minimizes a distorted perception of the world with the thought that the realignment will make her happier.

While I here refrain from identifying this psychological difficulty with any particular thinker or school of thought, I do think it is close to some common beliefs about a troubled mind, about what should be done to cure the problem, and the fashion in which it presupposes that one can construct a different conception of the self. Admittedly, we have been characterizing here experiences that differ widely, ranging from the adoption of a personality trait and the development of career plans to a religious conversion experience and response to neurosis. Yet, in each case we can see the relevance of our theory of human nature. In each case we presupposed that individuals can choose what they become and that their choice entails rules for conduct. Put differently, consider the unlikelihood of our coming upon one who asserts that he or she is or wants to become of such and such a nature but denies that either the status or the becoming at all governs his or her present actions. This study brings out how closely tied an account of self-construction is to rule-guided activity, the second important claim in our analysis of human nature. It is this claim that we must now investigate in more detail.

FURTHER DEVELOPMENT AND REFINEMENT OF THE VIEW: OUR RULE-GUIDED NATURE

A few further comments about this aspect of our view of human nature are in order. First, it may seem paradoxical to say, on the one hand, that one can construct one's essence, but that, on the other, a fixed aspect of one's nature or essence is that one is rule-guided. Suppose one should construct a view of human nature that precludes one's being rule-guided? My response here would be that any conception that is constructed would suggest to the person the parameters, wide or narrow, within which he or she can or should act, and to that extent one's conception has thereby set out some rules of conduct. One who, for example, asserts the superiority of the will over reason and decides to overrule any dictates suggested by reason that conflict with the will's promptings will at least have set down one rule—namely, to ignore the urgings of reason when the will pulls in another direction. Going beyond this limiting case, however, we can find numerous views of humans as essentially rule-guided.

Prominent among psychologists who portray people as rule-guided in their moral lives are Kohlberg and Piaget—among philosophers, Kant and C. I. Lewis. These psychologists tend to take it as a given that humans are rule-guided, and their contribution mainly involves a description of the development of the rule-guided being.

Apparently the truth of the thesis regarding our rule-guided nature becomes obvious upon our being presented with the particular descriptive account. Lewis, who at one point suggests that the test for the correctness of a theory of human nature is simply our own affirmation of the truth of some account, seems to endorse this approach of the psychologists. After a brief look at these approaches, I wish to extend this work by arguing for the correctness of the view that humans are rule-guided, drawing, in particular, on some of Lewis's insights.

Contributions from Psychology

Kohlberg is now well known for his identification of six stages in the moral development of the human. His findings are based on surveys conducted around the world—in the United States, Great Britain, Turkey, Taiwan, the Yucatan. In his investigations, he elicited responses to a moral problem in which a man, after pursuing unsuccessfully other alternatives, breaks into a drug store to obtain a drug to save his wife's life. Kohlberg found that the responses fell into roughly six discrete categories and that there was a correlation between the age of the person giving the response and the type of answer the person gave, leading Kohlberg to suspect that the categories could be structured as stages of moral development.

At the first stage, the child is oriented towards the avoidance of punishment and an unquestioning deference to power. Kohlberg makes no reference at this stage to any understanding on the part of the child of right and wrong action. At the second stage the right action is perceived as what satisfies one's own needs; the third, what conforms to the expectation of the various groups of which the individual is a member; the fourth, as doing one's duty with an orientation toward fixed rules and the maintenance of the social order; the fifth, what is agreed upon by the society as furthering social utility; and the sixth, what accords with self-chosen ethical principles capable of universal application and with a respect for the dignity of human beings as individuals.[23]

Now, there are a number of senses in which we can attribute to Kohlberg a rule-guided account of the human qua moral agent. For one thing, Kohlberg tells us that, even during the early stages of development, the agent dimly perceives the nature of justice as one that requires principled action. So at the early stages, on this account, we might say the agent is developing into the rule-guided agent. Second, during stages two through six, we are told the agent has a sense of right and wrong action. To the extent we recognize right and wrong as being a function of whether some act conforms to a rule of action, even at these stages, we can say the agent's act is principled. And third, we do find explicit reference to the agent's following rules in stages four, five, and six.

Contrasting with Kohlberg's linear development of the agent is Piaget's notion that two distinct and concurrent lines of development are traceable in the child's moral development. One, with four stages, has to do with the application of rules; the other, with three stages, with the "consciousness" of rules. One thing that becomes readily apparent is that rules figure prominently in Piaget's account of development, and there is no question of the rule-guided nature of this phenomenon. Moreover, his studies of children learning game rules deal with the use of rules in experience generally and not just moral experience.

In the stages of the application of rules, the first is characterized by rules reflecting habitual activity or "ritualized schemas" based on the child's desires. The second phase in this development, occurring between ages two and five, Piaget calls egocentric. Here, although the child is aware of external, codified rules that others may use, his or her use is strictly individual. Between seven and eight, the child enters the "stage of incipient cooperation."[24] A concern with the rules' applying to everyone and of mutual control enters at this level, although, Piaget says, the apprehension of the rules is vague. The vagueness dissipates at stage four, when the child is between eleven and twelve, and hence the stage is known as "that of the codification of rules."[25] As for the development of the consciousness of rules, Piaget tells us that, in the first stage, rules lack any coercive character; in the second, they are perceived as immutable; in the third, as alterable given their perceived foundation in mutual consent.[26] The second stage occurs between ages two and five and the third, between six and twelve.[27]

Contributions from Philosophy

Some philosophers depict humans as rule-guided and do so with no more of an independent concern for establishing a connection between rules and our nature than some psychologists. Portraying humans as autonomous, givers of laws unto themselves, Kant may also be seen as a thinker in this vein of seeing humans as rule-guided. Rational agents, free to formulate rules governing their situations and to force themselves to follow them upon convincing themselves of their willingness for them to have universal applicability, are, in effect, formulators and followers of rules.[28] And to the extent that depicting humans as rational beings is Kant's primary comment on human nature, we can recognize clearly the rule-guided character of human nature on the Kantian view.

Nonetheless, important differences between this and the view we are urging here should be noted. Kant requires consistency—whether the rational being is willing for anyone to follow the rule he or she is considering to follow. In short, one might say that a rule so universalized is one that is rational or ought to be followed by a rational being. And, as a rational being, one might recognize that such a rule is the obvious normative advice that would follow from one's seeing oneself as a rational being and recognizing as one's general directive "Be rational" or "Act rationally." But note that, on the Kantian view, that is the only fashion in which rules are tied to our nature. To the extent that one is a rational being, one is, in effect, to act rationally. While our view allows for one's portraying oneself as a rational being with rationality perhaps as a preeminent quality, it allows for more latitude in the construction of our nature and, as will become apparent, for more guidance in the ways in which rules are tied to the various ingredients of this construction.

The American philosopher C. I. Lewis pursued the development of an ethical theory by considering the general rule-guided nature of humans and subsumed them as ethical agents under that more general conception. His work in ethics is especially interesting in that, on the one hand, he saw as a motivation for his earlier works in logic, epistemology, and value theory the construction of an ethical theory; yet when he died, his project was incomplete, his shelves being "lined with dozens of notebooks, containing innumerable drafts and studies for his final work" in ethics.[29] His work in ethics, in a sense, then, leaves us with some insights still in need of reflection and refinement, and it is here, I think, that we can follow up fruitfully with additional argumentation designed to establish our rule-guided nature.

Three aspects of Lewis's theorizing are particularly relevant. First, Lewis develops a general, pragmatic thesis concerning the interrelatedness of knowledge and action with his view of statements of objective fact. For the human mind, we find that any objective claim, like "The stove is hot," materially implies an infinite number of supporting tests, like "If you touch the stove, you will be burned," and parallel pieces of advice for the direction of action, like "If you don't want to be burned, don't touch the stove."[30] By Lewis's view, the apprehension of objective facts is simultaneously the apprehension of imperatives for conduct, with each being different modes for expressing the same slice of experience. In effect, structuring our experience in terms of rules for future conduct is as natural for us as structuring our experience in terms of objective facts. Another aspect of Lewis's theory reveals how Lewis rests our being rule-guided on *observations* of human nature. His view is that our nature is not something we can show with an argument but something we can observe. I try to extend this approach by showing how these observations fit into an argument for our being rule-guided. Let us begin by considering Lewis's treatment of a question he raises: "Why rules?". One of Lewis's answers to the question revolves around our inability to govern our behavior in any other way, which Lewis speaks of, at one point, as a fact that can be observed.[31] According to Lewis:

Men can direct their action to foreseeable ends only by reference to some explicit or implicit generality—because they can
do nothing in this world except by applying to the present or
future something learned in the past, and this is possible with
respect to a newly presented or anticipated situation only so far
as it is subsumable in some class with past like cases. We know
how to bring about what we can expect to happen in the present
case only because it is what has happened in past like instances.
In consequence, a directive which failed to have such generality—failed to be of the form "In cases such-and-such, do so-and-
so"—would be quite impossible for any human mind to frame
or utilize. We act according to some implicitly formulatable rule
or we do not direct our action to foreseeable ends at all.[32]

In attempting to further Lewis's observations about human
nature, we should first note that some of what Lewis is saying here
about humans may first be stated more abstractly as characteristics
of the nature of rule-guided activity or of what we mean by certain
key concepts involved with such activity, making no reference yet to
human beings:

1. If one applies the past to present or foreseeable future
ends to direct one's action, one must classify aspects of the
present or future with the past to direct one's action.
2. If one directs one's action by classifying aspects of the
present or future with the past, one is acting in accord with
implicit or explicit directives of doing (rules).

At this point we might enter some of Lewis's portrayal of
human nature from the quotation above:

3. Humans direct their action by applying the past to present or foreseeable future ends.

From (1) and (3) we get:

4. Hence, humans must classify aspects of the present or future with the past.

And from (2) and (4) we get:

5. Hence, humans act in accord with implicit or explicit directives of doing (rules).

What we end up with is an argument that allows us to show that human activity is essentially rule-guided without starting off with a characterization of human activity as being such.

In addition to Lewis's observation of human nature and the argument we developed from it, his works also suggest that we are rule-guided creatures by pointing to the absurd situation the rule skeptic is in. The rule skeptic seemingly wants to convince us that there are no rules guiding our evaluations of right and wrong, yet in trying to show the correctness of the view, that he or she is *right*, he or she presupposes that there are such things as right and wrong.[33]

Besides seeing the absurdity that the skeptic is in when he or she denies that humans are rule-guided, we can also, it seems, extend Lewis's strategy. We can turn to human experience generally and find that broad areas of it are reduced to the unintelligible when it is assumed that humans are not rule-guided. Consider our sense that we ourselves lay down rules for our conduct and follow them, that we teach children, students, and adults rules, and that they conform their acts to them. Witness the phenomena of people's playing games, complying with the dictates of a legal system, learning a language. Again, it seems we end up in an awkward position if we cannot lend credence to the occurrence of such phenomena.

The foregoing study of psychologists and philosophers who have entertained views of humans as rule-guided can be seen as serving a variety of purposes. For one thing, we can see how some leading accounts of moral development and conduct require a thesis of our rule-guidedness for the theory to unfold; for Kohlberg and Piaget the thesis seems so evident that its truth can be safely assumed without the need of explicit endorsement. Further, we observed how Lewis's undertaking to argue for the thesis, even though he himself was sympathetic with its being self-evident, created opportunities for us to develop and refine his project. In effect, we were able to provide some independent grounds for establishing the rule-guided nature of humans. Having done so, we have completed the second part of our task of making plausible our view of humans as the constructors of rule-referring conceptions of their nature, the first focusing on the construction itself.

If we accept that our most general identity of being human is subject to our construction, we are not far from recognizing that our specific roles are too. We have already acknowledged how legal ethics develops conceptions of attorneys. We can see this activity of legal ethics now as an instance of, or analogous to, our more general project of developing a view of human nature. On this model, our construction of any of our specific roles is an instance of, or analogous to, our more general project. And in the absence of any reasons for thinking that any of our particular roles defy the construction which the attorney's role lends itself to, we can think of them as indeed open to our construction. More simply, we might accept that our particular roles are subject to our construction by including within the scope of human nature our nature relative to specific roles we occupy.

RAW MATERIALS FOR THE CONSTRUCTION

Let us now turn to the issue of what we are to draw on to construct a view of our nature or of our nature relative to particular roles we occupy. As for the raw materials from which to choose, I point to the ideas or phenomena that underlie the various issues surrounding what it is to be human, a professional, a mother, a lawyer, and so on. For example, with regard to whether we choose to see ourselves as self-interested or social, we can say that this particular competition presents a value issue, with the ideas or phenomena of being self-interested or social underlying the issue and being the raw materials from which to choose in constructing a view of our nature. The particular choice that is made both creates a value and shows what we do value. Indeed it would be odd to say that one chose to see oneself as self-interested but that one valued the contrary quality or that one's choice shows that one values some contrary value. The scope of the issues surrounding each conception to be constructed is best described as the category of relevant issues. This description, on the one hand, allows us latitude for the construction, but, on the other, imposes bounds that show the class of qualities is not arbitrary—whether we want to conceive of ourselves as having feathers is irrelevant.

As for what we may draw on for the construction, we may see fellow persons and what we learn about them through first- and second-hand experiences as providing a vast storehouse of possibilities of human behavior and thus of what one may seek to employ or avoid in a construction of self. People who are, or portrayals of people who are niggardly or generous, of those kindly and sensitive to the needs of others and of those inured to pain and suffering; people who are, or depictions of people who are, heroes and saints, martyrs, and rogues; the ways of members of our sub-cultures, of other cultures, and of criminal elements and the revelations of these in works of fiction, history, and the social sciences—all serve as grist for our choices. As we have direct contact with these possibilities or as presentations are made to us of such possibilities, we at once have made real for us qualities to imitate or eschew, and, as we do so, we engage in our construction of self. As the equanimity of *Wuthering Heights'* narrator, Nelly Dean, is brought into sharp contrast with the ugliness of Heathcliff's rages and inhuman vindictiveness, the reader both understands the nature of the choice and, to the extent that the issue is relevant for ongoing dealings with others, chooses and contributes to the development of self. To the extent that our own experiences with others are broad and rich enough to allow us to encounter such possibilities, those too can be seen as sources for the construction.

Why we choose one way or another is a matter addressed by a number of theorists of human nature. If anything general can be found in these thinkers, it is that the values we choose are relative to human desires that are the invariable, outer bounds limiting what we can value. As we shall see, while these accounts may restrict our choice of values, they do not preclude a choice. Rejecting what he considers the dominant, rational model of the human moral agent, Richard Taylor portrays that which we term good and evil in terms of our pursuit of the objects of our desires.[34] Casting the matter in the language of genetics, another commentator is able to subsume the phenomenon of human valuings under a more general and uniform description concerning animal species and their "genetic preference patterns": "Humans are members of an animal species, have a genetically determined pattern of feelings, and therefore have a species value system."[35] Attempting to keep in perspective the biological or evolutionary accounts of human values, Florian von Schilcher and Neil Tennant argue that "evolutionary theory...is not being pressed into service as the sole premise from which values are being derived.... All it does is make us more mindful of the *given* in human nature, the reasons why it *is* given, and the limits of the human condition as such."[36] The point that emerges for our further deliberations about selecting among values to construct conceptions of ourselves is this: the recent and growing literature on the genetic basis of our value constructions does not preclude our debating with ourselves or others about which to select when there is a competition of values or our ultimately choosing among rival values. The choice between being self-interested or social may be a choice between two values each of which may have a genetic foundation. But that does not mean that the choice itself is determined or that there is no choice available.

More should be said now about the product of our choices or of the constructed conception. As with any facet of our considered understanding of our world, we can see our concept of ourselves as a dynamic one, subject to change as new experiences bring with them suggestions for reevaluation and modification. The public service attorney inclined to revise a commitment to render aid to the poor in the face of the ingratitude of his or her clientele and small wages is much like the scientist refining or reformulating a hypothesis on the effect of the emission of ionizing radiation into the atmosphere in the light of increasing evidence of its long-range, harmful consequences. Moreover, we strive to make consistent the ingredients of our constructed view of ourselves, again, much as we order other domains of our experience. We perceive a powerful tension in a commitment to see ourselves as both self-interested and social, and we strive to harmonize the two or to surrender one, seeing the rejected value perhaps as one held through self-deception.[37] And this is little different from our efforts to reconcile our teachings and commitments coming from a religion with those from science as they sometimes collide. Nor is it essentially different from our efforts to make compatible various conflicting interests that are the subject of our laws, like the interests to drive rapidly on the highways, to save lives, and to conserve our fossil-fuel resources.

The motivation for all of this, I gather, is to eliminate the inconsistent or contradictory. To the extent that matters will seem better once the infelicity is somehow reconciled, the motivation is one of making things better. So closely tied to this process of reevaluating how we understand ourselves and our world is an interest in creating effective understandings, which is demonstrated in part by our interest in making our beliefs cohere. Our general commitment to forming good constructions is also evident, I think, from the incongruity we see in one's willingness to construct a notion of human nature or of some role which the constructor knows to be less useful or worse than other readily available alternatives. Further, as we build our conceptions and act in a world where role modeling is a reality, we acknowledge our willingness for others to imitate us and thereby strengthen our endorsement of our constructions.

PRACTICAL APPLICATION OF THIS THEORY
FOR LEGAL ETHICS AND FOR THE ATTORNEY

What more concretely can be said about all of this for one's constructing a conception of an attorney and its relevance for legal

ethics? As we will see in the next chapter, there are a number of factors that various commentators have identified for our understanding what a profession is, and for understanding law as a profession,
and we can turn to these as the raw materials for these particular
constructions. We will see that, often, reasonable debate surrounds
their inclusion in the concept of a professional or a lawyer. Thus, one
attorney, employing a critical attitude, may decide to see himself or
herself as autonomous, a critic of culture, and primarily profit-ori-
ented, as regards a few of the variables that will be discussed.
Another may concur on some of these variables and disagree with or
be silent on others as he or she engages in the construction. The person who has chosen to be or become, as part of the conception, a
critic of culture, *should* seize and create opportunities for doing so
lest the choice be vacuous. Or turn to the issue regarding attorneys'
knowledge and the extent to which that separates them from other
workers. Here too we will see how varying conceptions about what
the nature of the lawyer's knowledge and skills are suggest normative advice and hence the important interrelationship we have been
urging between our constructed conceptions and rules for conduct.[38]

Let us consider just this element of knowledge and skills for further illustration and elucidation. On the one hand, drawing in part on
the values of efficiency, accuracy, and certainty, one might think of the
attorney's nature, in part, as that of a skilled technician who can guide
his or her client through the complex workings of a legal system that is
elusive to the common mind, as one who, well-versed in the law,
effects intricate and logically compelling solutions to the problems of
his or her client. We might follow Fuller in the further construction of
this view, indicating that the law this attorney deals with is seen basically as fixed and given, awaiting the attorney's discovery of his or her
client's rights.[39] So conceived, we might reasonably suggest that the
attorney ought not to be arguing the rightness of the client's cause,
reaching for extra-legal principles in so arguing, but rather that the
attorney ought, and here further normative advice enters, to argue the
rights of the client based, again, on the attorney's analytical working
out of the client's problem against the backdrop of the extant laws.

On the other hand, drawing in part on the values of progress, flexibility, and intelligibility, as well as to general fairness and justice, one might think of the attorney as one who knows well the fundamental guiding ideals of the legal order and keeps them always in mind as he or she considers options open to the client and as he or she views the legal system, always mindful of the essential connection between the legal rule and the ideal. Within such a view, technical and mechanistic determinations of the rights of the client as per the existing laws are not first in order, but rather, the attorney ought to be arguing the rightness of the client's cause, again, appealing to factors like the goals, purposes, and ideals of the legal order.

These are but examples of how we might proceed, neither representing a total conception of the attorney's nature nor even necessarily desirable conceptions. The attempt has been one of illustrating how there are choices for constructing an adequate or fruitful conception of the attorney and of how, based on that conception, we might suggest norms, moral and nonmoral, for the guidance of the attorney's conduct.

What becomes evident is that our general theory of human nature, which lies at the foundation of legal ethics and whose development resulted from our pursuing the desirable features of legal ethics, now allows us to enrich legal ethics. It makes explicit the necessity of lawyers' acquainting themselves with the dimensions of themselves as professionals and as attorneys for their project of critically assessing their nature and laying down rules for ethical conduct. To further this end, we turn in the next chapter to a study of the elements that seem likely and useful for building these conceptions.

MAGRITTE, Rene. *The Rights of Man.* 1945. Oil, 57-1/2 x 44-7/8" © 1992
ARS, N.Y./ADAGP, Paris.

3

▼

Professions and the Legal Profession

PURPOSE OF THE INQUIRY

"The essence of a profession is that the measure of success is the service performed and not the gains amassed."[1] "A profession... refers to a group of men pursuing a learned art in the spirit of public service."[2] "A profession is a self-disciplined group of individuals who hold themselves out to the public as possessing a special skill, derived from training or education, and who are prepared to exercise that skill primarily for the interest of others."[3]

Thus run a few of the numerous attempts to define a profession. That considerable energies have been expended to define a profession no one questions. Typical among the comments on the literature is "academic scholars have devoted uncounted hours to the definition and characterization of professions."[4] Some seem to think little of all this study. Says one commentator, "This excessive concern with specifying and respecifying the 'essentials' of professionalism has resulted in several related factors which have kept research on professionalism in a comparatively embryonic state."[5] For others, the project is perceived as tiresome, but nonetheless the question raised is considered worthwhile: "While the usage of the word is

67

highly confused, and its definition for purposes both of scholarship and social accounting a matter of wearisome debate, the phenomena addressed are of very special theoretical and practical importance."[6] Comments are also found that place a uniformly favorable gloss on the literature, bringing out that "many decades of sociological research and writing have produced a rich literature dealing with occupational roles."[7]

As we have seen, for our purposes, one very practical reason for continuing to press these inquiries is to acquaint professionals with the variables involved for their constructing a view of themselves as a professional and, for our special interest here in the legal profession, with the nature of the lawyer qua professional. In general, this approach is foreign to the literature, since each analyst typically determines what the professional role entails and then assigns the role so conceived to the professional. Our approach invites professionals to adopt an attitude that they are competent to use this literature as grist for the construction of their roles and to break from any attitude that would interfere with this constructive endeavor.

Actually, three major attitudes with regard to occupying some particular role[8] or status can be distinguished. Only the third is consistent with the theory of human nature we developed and with how we are calling upon professionals, or people in any role, to act. The first attitude, call it the "unreflective attitude," is exemplified where, because of the situation one finds oneself in, one accepts the status thereby conferred *simpliciter*. For example, the man or the woman, because of the situation he or she is in of having biologically reproduced, takes this situation as a sufficient characterization of himself or herself in the role of a father or a mother. Compare this with the next attitude, call it the "partially reflective attitude," where an attempt is made to understand what is entailed by this status—the expectations, obligations, and associations it carries with it. Here, the individual will attempt to acquire knowledge about the role, perhaps through recollection of experiences with his or her own parents, through inquiry and exchanges of information, thereby gaining an understanding of the role to guide future actions. The literature on what a profession is generally panders to this attitude in that each contributor presents his or her analysis as definitive for a full understanding of what a profession is.

The final attitude, the "critical attitude," goes further than the second in that the collected wisdom of, say, fatherhood is not simply turned to, assimilated, and used as a guide for the direction of one's activity within this role. Rather, what one employing the critical attitude does is familiarize oneself with the information available and, upon reflection, construct in an ongoing process what one considers to be the best conception to guide one's actions. This advice might be seen as nothing more than a spin-off of the familiar dictum concerning the poverty of the unreflective existence, but, more to the point here, an unwillingness to embrace the critical attitude seems symptomatic of a willingness to cast off one's ability to self-govern and to ignore our nature as constructors of rule-referring conceptions of our nature and our roles. Considerations of this sort, I take it, point to the value of carefully considering and analyzing the literature on what a profession is and on law as a profession—that professionals themselves might be assisted in critically assessing their roles and constructing conceptions of themselves and that the general reader be provided with a sustained example or paradigm case of how one can make inquiries relevant to the construction of a conception.

METHODOLOGIES FOR DETERMINING
WHAT A PROFESSION IS

In what follows, an attempt is made to make explicit the alternative, methodological approaches that can be employed in answering the question of how we should conceive of the nature of something. A number of these approaches, as we will see, have been employed, commented on, or evaluated in the literature on what a profession is, and it is these that we will primarily focus on. All in all this focus should allow us both to factor out of the literature qualities relevant to constructing a conception without distorting the environment in which the investigator presented them and to make clear how our project that urges a construction differs from and is better than other approaches. First, however, let us at least identify a complete range of methodologies for determining something's nature in the spirit of creating the broader context for our discussions: (Readers unconcerned with this discussion of methodologies should proceed directly to the discussion of the significant features of a profession in the next section.)

1.   One may search for the necessary and sufficient conditions of some concept.

2.   One may be interested in describing how some word, in fact, is used by a group of speakers.

3.   One may attempt to go beyond the ordinary usage of some word and to describe with greater care some thing or phenomenon, making no normative claims of how we ought to employ some phenomenon or word.

4.   One may be interested in setting forth an understanding of some word or phenomenon by looking to its purpose or function, setting out a purposive definition.

5.   One may be interested in providing an analysis whereby clear instances of common usage are tests of a successful analysis, but the analysis itself provides a test for distinguishing situations in common usage considered to be unclear.

6.   One may recognize that matters of degree are important in isolating what is distinctive and turn to some scale or continuum.

7.   One may find it useful to bifurcate our understanding of some concept into some ideal and real world.

8.   One may turn to what a thing has been, its history, to understand what it is.

Of these, perhaps the approach mentioned most in the current literature about professions is (6), which employs a continuum. One commentator introduces this approach by pointing to some of the difficulties with the standard technique of determining the necessary and sufficient conditions suggested in (1). Bayles points out that the difficulty with the search for the necessary and sufficient conditions of a profession is the large variety of professions that must be accounted for by the general analysis:

> One need not characterize professions by a set of necessary and sufficient features possessed by all professions and only by professions. The variety of professions is simply too great for that approach. Rather, some features can be taken as necessary for an occupation to be a profession, and others as simply common to many professions and as raising similar ethical concerns.[9]

At this point Bayles draws the reader's attention to the work of Moore and to the possibility of employing a continuum as set out in (6) above. Using this type of approach, another commentator, Greenwood, tells us that

> the true difference between a professional and a non-professional occupation is not a qualitative but a quantitative one. Strictly speaking, these attributes are not the exclusive monopoly of the professions; non-professional occupations also possess them, but to a lesser degree.... As is true of most social phenomena, the phenomenon of professionalism cannot be structured in terms of clear cut classes. Rather, we must think of the occupations in a society as distributing themselves along a continuum. At one end of this continuum are bunched the well-recognized and undisputed professions (e.g., physician, attorney, professor, scientist); at the opposite end are bunched the least skilled and least attractive occupations (e.g., watchman, truckloader, farm laborer, scrubwoman, bus boy).... The occupations bunched at the professional pole of the continuum possess to a maximum degree the attributes....[10]

Barber seems to concur in this approach, indicating that what he identifies as the essential attributes, which we will consider below, "define a scale of professionalism, a way of measuring the extent to which it is present in different forms of occupational performance."[11] Says Barber, "The most professional behavior would be that which realizes all four attributes in the fullest possible manner."[12] Further, focusing on Barber's methodology, we find the means by which he arrived at these attributes; he tells us that "a sociological definition of the professions should limit itself, so far as possible, to the *differentia specifica* of professional behavior. For example, concepts like style of life, corporate solidarity, and socialization structures and processes, which apply to all other groups as well as to professional ones, are not the *differentia specifica*."[13]

Since this model of employing a scale or continuum is so pervasive in the literature, what needs to be investigated is the clarity of this model. First, while it may follow from the supposition that we can compare occupations on a simple scale, that the difference between professional and nonprofessional occupations is quantitative, it is not at all clear that a single scale can be used. Suppose what were isolated as the essential attributes of a profession were attributes A, B, C, and D. Presumably we would have a scale of occupations ranging from those seemingly nonprofessional to those professional or very professional. Thus we might have

Security guard —————————— *Medical doctor*
Occupations

This scale/continuum itself makes some sense, given that it reflects our intuition that both the security guard and the medical doctor have an occupation and, further, that the security guard is not a professional whereas the medical doctor clearly is. But it suggests that we should expect some single variable, professionalism, to be increasing as we move along the continuum, an expectation that conflicts with the starting point of these analyses, that a number of attributes—say, A, B, C, and D—are operative.

Moreover, it seems the use of the continuum, along which several factors vary, would lead us to make some unusual pronouncements. Let me make this clearer. Suppose with regard to the essential attributes A, B, C, D, each varying from 1 to 100, occupation X registers A=1, B=30, C=5, D=60, and occupation Y registers A=0, B=0, C=0, D=100. It seems we would have to place occupation Y farther on the continuum than X even though Y displays only one of the essential attributes for what a profession is while X has all four present. Even without looking at concrete examples, we can already begin to detect certain counter-intuitive results arising from using a continuum, which by its nature suggests the increase of a single variable but is here being used to gauge a variety of variables. More generally, the model of the scale or continuum does not seem adequate to carry the conceptual weight involved. And if one resorts simply to claiming that only professionalism is increasing, then we end up leaving unanalyzed what we were after. So it seems that the analysis of the essential attributes of a profession must be freed from this model of the continuum/scale if we are to preserve the clarity of the project.

Let us now turn to Cullen's decription of his basic procedure for understaning professionalism:

> Taking several ideal-typical definitions of professionalism as variable-identifiers, the basic procedure was to examine the interrelationship among selected occupational characteristics. That is, no particular set of occupational features was considered as representing the definition of professionalism.[14]

Further, Cullen tells us that there are two rival explanations of the nature of professionalism, which he wishes to assess in the light of empirical studies. One approach explains the development of an occupation into a profession in terms of the occupation's needing certain qualities intrinsic to a profession's nature, like long training and ethical codes.[15] The other approach points to the occupational group's motive to acquire the power of the professionals as the explanation for attaining professionalism.[16]

Cullen's analysis, based on empirical studies, on a study of ideal-typical definitions, and on an evaluation of the competing theories mentioned above, leads him to distill one quality—intellectual complexity—as a fundamental feature of professionalism while at the same time giving credence to the significance of group power in accounting for professionalism:

> Based on current United States data, the result of this quantita-
> tive occupational study indicated that for the most part, the
> characteristics usually associated with high degrees of profes-
> sionalism...emerge largely from a greater intellectual complex-
> ity of occupational tasks.... However, intrinsic occupational tal-
> ent is not the sole reason for the existence of professionalism's
> various characteristics. Once intellectual complexity's effects
> were held constant, the results also showed that occupational
> group power increases the ability to attain professionalism's
> elements and to reap the attendant rewards.[17]

As numerous as the variety of approaches Cullen draws on in his analysis are the attendant confusions surrounding his method. More specifically, it seems that a host of analytically separable issues are being dealt with concurrently in a fashion that creates the illusion that a problem is being solved when in fact a number of distinct issues need to be addressed. While they may be related, the issues of how an occupational group becomes a profession or attains professionalism, of what the characteristics of a profession or professionalism are, and of why some occupational group would want to attain professional status are not one and the same. It may be, for example, that a motivation to attain power accounts for why some occupational group seeks professional status but figures little in their actually achieving that status, such hinging, perhaps, on the nature of the service provided.

As we have seen, many investigators of the issue of what a profession is have eschewed, wittingly or not, the strategy commonly employed by philosophers of formulating for some concept its necessary and sufficient conditions, here, for what a profession is. Accordingly, we found talk of identifying the essential features of a profession, of using scales or continua along which are work characteristics, some of which some professions possess to a higher degree than others, of describing a phenomenon, or of employing ideal-typical definitions that need not be seen as deficient should our experience deviate. Further, we identified difficulties that attend these methodologies.

Now, I, too, am not certain how important it is to search for the necessary and sufficient conditions for a profession or to establish the impossibility of doing so, so long as we can isolate features of a profession that roughly fall into such categories as "highly significant for understanding what a profession is." This approach allows us to review those features identified by a variety of analyses, to evaluate them critically, and to add to an enlightened understanding of the matter without falling into the trappings of claiming one to be a necessary condition only to be refuted later by some fanciful counter-example of a profession without this "necessary" feature. Moreover, as mentioned, this approach will allow us to pass more easily through the methodological approaches of different disciplines and to arrive at a contribution to this issue more catholic in nature than some while at the same time delivering up for us the raw materials for the informed and critical concept construction that we urge be undertaken. In a word, we will factor out of a longstanding and diverse literature material for a new purpose.

SIGNIFICANT FEATURES OF A PROFESSION

Let us now turn to an identification and evaluation of the distinctive elements commonly associated with a profession. These include there being: (1) special obligations to the public, (2) a body of specialized knowledge and skills that the members must acquire, (3) an orientation of service, (4) objects and practices symbolic of the work involved, (5) a special relationship between the members of the profession and their clients or patients, (6) a high degree of autonomy for the members, (7) expectations that its members assume roles of leadership, (8) a code of ethics, and (9) a professional association. As we move through a discussion of these features, I attempt to evaluate them critically with an eye more to making it clear what issues surround our endorsing these as features of a profession than to making a final determination that we must always, or never again, think of these as being characteristic of a profession. Such an approach, I believe, is consistent with our interest in encouraging one to exercise the critical attitude mentioned above insofar as the analysis presented here assists professionals and other interested parties in constructing a viable understanding of a profession and assists the general reader in learning by example something about the dynamics of role construction. As we saw with the development of a conception of human nature, the elements we include in the conception structure our conduct with rules, and this phenomenon of rules for conduct attending the constructed conception is no less present with the conceptions we construct of our roles. The person who conceives of the professional as a leader is committed to some general dictum to lead just as a person who conceives of the professional as a public servant is committed to a general dictum to subordinate the pursuit of profit to service. Let us now turn to a discussion of the candidates for inclusion in the concept of a profession.

Special Obligations

As we shall see, many of the attempts to isolate the key features of a profession posit rather plush catalogues of qualities. It is interesting to note that two of the sparsest characterizations both draw our attention to the fact that special obligations or responsibilities attach to members of a profession. Thus, we find in a report of an ABA joint conference on professional responsibility: "A profession to be worthy of the name must inculcate in its members a strong sense of the special obligations that attach to their calling."[18] Recognizing this, and with specific reference to the legal profession, it has been further remarked that "knowledge and skills gave the practitioner power. It was the point of view which determined whether the practitioner was going to use the power for well or ill, for himself or in the public interest. It was the recognition by lawyers of the importance of the point of view, or the degree of responsibility of the profession to the general public, which finally transformed the class into the profession."[19]

Alan Soble has argued for the position that nothing follows from the concept of a profession itself concerning the professional's obligations and that any obligations attributable to the professional should be based on considerations of social utility. Says Soble,

> One might say that it is important to determine what "profession" means and to be able to classify occupations as professional/nonprofessional because there are rights and duties attachable to professions that are not attachable to nonprofessions. This view is implicit in the...question, "Do professionals have the right...to advertise their services...?" But there is no advantage in asking the question in this fashion, and the terminology of "professionals" is mere deadweight. The important question is just whether it is advantageous, when all things are considered (the interests of the community, primarily), to allow those who provide medical and legal services to advertise. Nothing is gained by first asking whether those who do X ought to advertise, as if X's being a profession is itself somehow a morally significant fact that must be taken into account.[20]

In response to Soble, and consistent with the ABA's statement tying special obligations to knowledge, it has been brought out that, because professionals, by their nature, are in possession of "guilty knowledge," they do have special obligations that others do not. So let us pursue the issue of whether professionals, by their nature, have special obligations and do so in the context of their having this guilty knowledge. More specifically, guilty knowledge refers to information and skills, like how to remove an organ from a person, that, in a sense, is "dangerous" to know and which we expect most persons not to know. Occupations traditionally known as the professions specialize in this area of guilty knowledge. While possession of this knowledge for the ordinary person makes him or her guilty, deviant or an object of our suspicion, such is not the case for the professional, and to be exempt from such attributions, the professional takes on special obligations. An example of one of these special obligations is that of controlling the education and supervision of novices.[21]

It might be noted that this notion of the professional's being set off from the common person because of special knowledge is not always cast in terms of knowledge of specific acts that can be performed, like the removal of an organ, but sometimes in terms of general intellectual powers that can open doors to wrongdoing:

> In short, in every profession where mental discipline and superior abilities raise a man above the level of the surrounding crowd, and equip him with extraordinary influence, the avenues of dishonesty and treachery are a thousand-fold increased.[22]

Further, the identification of the special responsibilities of the professional sometimes draws us into a consideration of other attributes identified as essential to understanding the nature of a profession, namely, codes and associations, which are used to supervise all members of the group to ensure that this knowledge mentioned above has been obtained and employed properly.

A few observations are in order to put in perspective this debate over whether professionals, by their nature, have special obligations. On the one hand, these special obligations may attach because of the peculiarities of the professional's knowledge, which is part of what we mean by a profession; thus, there is something inherently normative about the concept of a profession, and these special obligations follow from it. But it may also be that the concept itself is silent on obligation, which is determined independently on the basis of social utility. Even so, the nature of guilty knowledge, for example, may be such that the interest of the community always weighs on the side of positing a special obligation; arguably, the public would always want to safeguard itself against those with this knowledge; put differently, considerations of social utility, on this line of reasoning, require that we assign an obligation regarding knowledge to the professionals, who, by their nature, have no such obligation. So it seems that, on either approach, if we are willing to attach the weight to this guilty knowledge that it seems to carry in assigning obligations, we can get the same result whether Soble's approach or the alternative is correct; we end up saying that those with this knowledge—professionals—do have special obligations.

Knowledge

Regardless of whether one sees the professional as having special obligations because of the possession of certain knowledge and skills, it nonetheless remains the case that this knowledge is usually pointed to as a distinguishing feature of a profession. Let us turn now to a closer look at the way in which knowledge may distinguish the professional. The following definition makes explicit the claim that a central feature of a profession is the special skills and knowledge peculiar to it; and this claim is brought out as our attention is drawn to the fact that other features are equally significant. Thus, Wright tells us that

> the factors to be considered in deciding if a calling is a profession are: the holding out to the public; the avowal of special skills; training and education; conscious community of interest as a self-disciplined group; and unselfishness. From these a modern meaning of a profession may be fashioned. A profession is a self-disciplined group of individuals who hold themselves out to the public as possessing a special skill, derived from training or education, and who are prepared to exercise that skill primarily for the interest of others. A professional person is a member of such a group.[23]

To underscore the necessity of knowledge being essential to conceiving a profession, Roscoe Pound points to a period of decline in the legal profession when there was a dilution of the knowledge requirement; he attributes this to the frontier mentality:

Both in idea and as a matter of history a profession is a learned profession; a body of learned men pursuing a learned art. The frontier idea which was expressed in the Constitution of Indiana in 1851—"Every person of good moral character, being a voter, shall be entitled to admission to practice law in all courts of justice"—is characteristic of the era of deprofessionalizing the professions.[24]

While Pound wishes to identify learning as central to what sets professions off from other occupations or crafts, he brings out that it is learning not just concerning the knowledge and skills requisite for entering some specific profession but also, it seems, some general learning indicative of what he calls the "cultivated intelligence":

Learning is one of the things which sets off a profession from a calling or vocation or occupation. Professions are learned not only from the nature of the art professed but historically have a cultural, an ideal, side which furthers the exercise of that art. Problems of human relations in society, problems of disease, problems of the upright life guided by religion are to be dealt with by the resources of cultivated intelligence by lawyer, physician, and clergyman. To carry on their tasks most effectively they must be more than resourceful craftsman. They must be learned men.[25]

Some commentators focus on how we can pinpoint the distinguishing features of the body of knowledge peculiar to a profession. In Greenwood's survey of studies isolating the significant features of professions, he concluded that "all professions seem to possess: (1) systematic theory, (2) authority, (3) community sanction, (4) ethical codes, and (5) a culture."[26] Of these, Greenwood points to the first as being crucial and elaborates: "The skills that characterize a profession flow from and are supported by a fund of knowledge that has been organized into an internally consistent system, called a body of theory. A profession's underlying body of theory is a system of abstract propositions that describe in general terms the classes of phenomena comprising the profession's focus of interest."[27]

Like Greenwood, Hughes seems to unpack the notion of the systematic theory in terms of its applicability to classes of cases that the profession deals with as distinct from some approach where the workers' interest is narrowed to dealing only with an individual case:

> In these examples appear the main themes of professionaliza-
> tion. Detachment is one of them; and that in the sense of having
> in a particular case no personal interest such as would influ-
> ence one's action or advice, while being deeply interested in all
> cases of the kind. The deep interest in cases is of the sort that
> leads one to pursue and systematize the pertinent knowledge.
> One aspect of a profession is a certain equilibrium between the
> universal and the particular.[28]

Whitehead strikes the distinction in a similar fashion but places emphasis on the dynamic interplay between the theoretical dimension of the professional's activities and the power of that dimension to alter subsequent activities of the professional. He speaks of a *craft* as "an avocation based upon customary activities and modified by the trial and error of individual practice." A *profession*, in contrast, is "an avocation whose activities are subjected to theoretical analysis, and are modified by theoretical conclusions derived from that analysis."[29]

While the foregoing characterizations of a profession explicitly introduce a cognitive component, this knowledge is instrumental in nature in that it is important to acquire for the purpose of effective practice. The next statement suggests that essential to a profession is knowledge that is pursued, in part, for its own sake: "As a member of a learned profession, a lawyer should cultivate knowledge of the law beyond its use for clients...."[30] Further, Wade brings out that

> there has been a consistent viewpoint that training is necessary
> to admission to a learned profession, and that the professions
> are based on an intellectual technique.... The organization
> exists primarily for the advancement of medicine, justice,
> teaching, not of the individual members, as in the case of trade
> unions.[31]

A relatively unproblematic feature of a profession, knowledge, has surrounding it an interesting and important question when we focus on whether professionals, by their nature, ought to pursue new knowledge for its own sake or for the advancement of the profession. In constructing a debate, let us consider, on the one side, that professors of law, medicine, dentistry, and engineering are the researchers of their respective fields, and it is part of their profession as educators that makes essential not just the transmission of knowledge but also the discovery and application of new knowledge. Further, general principles of division of labor exempt practitioners of law, medicine, etc., from these pursuits, for their task is one of using the knowledge they have acquired to solve pressing problems in daily practice. Countervailing considerations become apparent when we note the consequences of not requiring the professional to extend knowledge. First, it seems reasonable to assume that, during the course of practice, professionals will acquire first-hand experience with such things as the variance between the knowledge and techniques of their fields and what is needed to effect solutions, the most effective ways of handling recurring problems, and ways to improve delivery of service, to name a few. Not seeing themselves as discoverers of knowledge with an attendant responsibility to communicate this knowledge results in a failure for these discoveries to be objectified and made of use to the community.

In an important sense both of these arguments pull in extreme directions and do so unnecessarily. The first argument seems to wrongly assume that practice itself is not a laboratory for discovery, whereas the second argument just as wrongly assumes that the responsibility for communicating this knowledge gleaned from practice must vest solely in the practitioner. One way of resolving the matter is for theoreticians and practitioners each to conceive of themselves as discoverers and communicators of new knowledge, for each thereby to recognize an obligation to discover and communicate new knowledge, but for each to recognize that specific functions can then be allocated. Primary responsibility for informing theoreticians of discoveries and problems in practice would belong to the practitioner. Responsibility for pursuing the matter thoroughly might be assigned primarily to the theoretician.

Service

That professionals and people in business both make profits, no one denies; yet they are worlds apart, in the end, when we recognize, on the one hand, that professionals' profits do not result from the trading of material goods and, on the other, that professionals' pursuit of profit is supposed to be subordinate to the spirit of service with which they perform their tasks. Says Carr-Saunders, concerning the former:

> the position of the fee-taking professional is in some respects analogous to that of the manufacturer or dealer.... there remains, however, the profound distinction that manufacturers and dealers do, whereas professional men do not, buy and sell material goods as an essential feature in the performance of their functions. This distinction is so important that, however closely the organization of some professions may come to resemble business organization and however much specialized study and training in relation to these functions may come to be characteristic of the manufacturer or dealer, there can be no transformation of one into the other.[32]

In paving the way for introducing service as essential in striking the distinction between business and the professions, Roscoe Pound first brings out that, for the professional, earning a livelihood, and hence the pursuit of profit, is neither an important consideration, as in other walks of life, nor is it primary, as in business:

> But while in all walks of life men must bear this in mind, in business and trade it is the primary purpose. In a profession, on the other hand, it is an incidental purpose, pursuit of which is held down by traditions of a chief purpose to which the organized activities of those pursuing the calling are to be directed primarily, and by which the individual activities of the practitioner are to be restrained and guided.[33]

Having discounted the pursuit of profit as primary ·for the professional, Pound then points to public service as a profession's main
purpose:

> By a profession, such as the ministry, medicine, law, teaching,
> we mean much more than a calling which has a certain tradi-
> tional dignity and certain other callings which in recent times
> have achieved or claim a like dignity. There is much more in a
> profession than a traditionally dignified calling. The term refers
> to a group of men pursuing a learned art as a common calling
> in the spirit of public service because it may incidentally be a
> means of livelihood. Pursuit of the learned art in the spirit of a
> public service is the primary purpose.[34]

Although many analysts, like Pound, see service as seminal in
articulating what a profession stands for, Pound does so, it is interesting to note, in such a fashion that we see how other central qualities of a profession—knowledge and organization—can be seen as
hinging on service. Says Pound,

> It is the essence of a profession that it is practiced in a spirit of
> public service.... The other two elements of a profession,
> namely, organization and pursuit of a learned art, have their
> justification in that they secure and maintain that spirit.[35]

Few could fail to perceive a tension between the way the world
is and a definition of a profession that distinguishes a profession from
a business or a trade on the ground that the members of a profession
operate in the spirit of performing a service as against the pursuit of
profit by the person in business. We know that, with regard to law, its
early practitioners were frequently men of independent wealth who
did not practice for profit but to perform a service. This association of
the profession with service arguably became a ground for many commentators seeing service as an essential ingredient of the profession.
On the other hand, we find analyses that have so divested themselves
of these past associations that public service attorneys are sometimes

described as wanting to return to the traditional notion of the professional, indicating that an orientation of service simply does not fit our
current understanding of the professional.[36]

Useful in clarifying the issue is a distinction between the motive
for performing some activity and its effect. Thus, concerning profit
and service, one may, motivated by profit, pursue an activity with an
effect being that the agent reaps profit. Or, with the same profit
motive, one might find only service resulting from the activity, or both
service and profit. On the other hand, action motivated by service, or
done in the spirit of service, may result in service, profit, or both. And
activity motivated by service and profit may have similar consequences. Now, if, in some way, the profit/service distinction is to be
useful in distinguishing the professional from the person in business,
how should the distinction be cast, given the range of these variables?

It is not at all clear that the motive is of primary significance as
it is in the traditional rendering of the distinction, where the attorney's work, for example, is said to be done in the spirit of public service. Consider an attorney whose acts are motivated solely by profit
and for whom the intent to provide some public service would be
quite foreign. Further, assume that the natural effect of this attorney's act is that such service is provided. Next, consider a person in
business who would like very much to render a service to the public,
indeed is so motivated, and because of this person's circumstances,
engages in a business practice that brings profit. To be sure, this
person also wants this profit and is motivated to acquire it. Yet, let
us assume there is no relevant sense in which this person's efforts
can be construed as rendering a service. Now, if, as those who would
have us focus on motive suggest, a motivation to serve is nobler than
that of reaping a profit, and in that motivation lies the ground for
distinguishing the professional from the person in business, we must
grant here that the person in business would triumph. Yet, I gather
that many would be unhappy with this result, for it diminishes the
practical significance of the lawyer's having provided, in fact, the
public service. Once this is conceded in this limiting case, it becomes
clear that, while one may wish to applaud the motive, what nonethe-

less, on this line of reasoning, remains essential in the estimation of the action is the effect—the rendering of the service.

The question now remains whether there is a significant sense in which we might recognize that the professions and their members tend to provide public service in the execution of their tasks and that the effect, in essence, is indeed one of providing public service. Arguably, the routine exercising of the doctor's or the lawyer's skills—the drafting of contracts, mortgages, and wills, the prescribing of antibiotics for a diagnosed infection, the filling of a cavity, or the removal of a ruptured appendix—all have the effect of providing important public services regardless of the motivation for doing them. In other words, the activities of professionals are essentially linked to the attainment of specific and significant social goods like health, justice, and education, whereas the activities of people in business are essentially linked only to profit and to no specific social good. The point is that if, in modern society, one finds professionals who do not subordinate the profit motive to that of public service, yet finds that public service is still a factor that sets the professional apart from the person in business, one may turn to the effect of the actions of members of these two groups to distinguish them; ultimately, one may focus on the likelihood of the professional's activity resulting in rendering a public service in contrast with that of the person in business and in this fashion strike the difference between the two in an attempt to construct a clear conception of the professional.

Symbols

Some writers have pointed to symbols as being central to understanding a profession. Barber, for example, speaks of these as "a system of rewards (monetary and honorary) that is primarily a set of symbols of work achievement and thus ends in themselves, not means to some end of individual self-interest."[37] Commenting on the values, norms, and symbols of the "culture of a profession," Greenwood says that symbols are the profession's "meaning-laden items. These may include such things as: its insignias, emblems, and distinctive dress; its history, folklore, and argot...."[38] I gather here we are to think of such things as the physicians's stethoscope and white coat, the judge's black robe and gavel, the pharmacist's mortar and pestle, perhaps a powdered wig of the barrister, folded newsprint and pencil of the journalist, typewriter of the writer, chalk of the teacher. "Publish or perish," "off the record," "reversed and remanded," "polish the apple," carry with them unmistakable associations, as do the levels of income we assume individuals make when we identify them as doctor, lawyer, journalist, teacher. And consider a folk story telling of the mysteries of the legal system, which compares taking one's legal problem to the law for a solution to taking one's grain to the public mill to be ground. The citizen turning to the law, the story suggests, is much like the farmer who is never sure what the particular fate of his bag of grain has been, whether the bag of ground flour corresponds to the bag of grain that went in.

Considerations of this sort seem to fall into the category of associations we make with particular professions rather than reveal the central features of any profession. The symbolic aspects of, say, law or medicine, to be sure, add to one's understanding of a particular occupation, but it is not clear that any generalization about professions having symbolic aspects would distinguish them from other occupations, events, or phenomena, which have such aspects by virtue of their simply being historical, human institutions. Consider the Boy Scout with his distinctive uniform, his motto of "be prepared," his ceremonial flags, and merit badges. Such symbols and argot, which arguably are more extensive in the Boy Scouts than in any particular profession, seem to say little about either professions or a group like the Boy Scouts except that they belong to a very general likeness class, namely, some human institution. If so, it seems that turning to symbols as an essential characteristic of professions, on this line of reasoning, is a move fraught with difficulties.

The Relationship between the Professional and the Client/Patient

That the professional and not the person the professional serves determines what is best for that person is a recurring theme in the literature distinguishing professions from occupations, and the distinction hinges on the professional's knowledge. Says Greenwood:

> A customer determines what services and/or commodities he wants and he shops around until he finds them.... In a professional relationship, however, the professional dictates what is good or evil for the client, who has no choice but to accede to professional judgment. Here the premise is that, because he lacks the requisite theoretical background, the client cannot diagnose his own needs or discriminate against the range of possibilities for meeting them.[39]

Goode underlines this, as he shows in what way the librarian falls short of being a professional:

> Intellectually, the librarian must work within the client's limitations instead of imposing his professional categories, conceptions, and authority on the client.... This strain between the wishes and the real needs of a clientele is perhaps to be found in all professions, but in established professions more often is it resolved by the professional's decision.[40]

Hughes' view on the matter is particularly interesting in that he weaves this idea of the professional's knowing what is best with a notion of *credat emptor*—let the buyer believe—and these with the idea that the professional has special knowledge: "A central feature, then, of all professions, is the motto...*credat emptor*.... The client is to trust the professional; he must tell him all secrets which bear upon the affairs in hand. He must trust his judgment and skill."[41]

All of the foregoing characterizations show professionals acting in the traditionally paternalistic fashion toward their patients or clients. Some recent studies bring out that the professional, arguably, is not bound to this model, that there are alternatives. If so, the upshot would be that acting in this paternalistic fashion is not an essential ingredient of what it is to be a professional. Other models that have been pursued and advocated include a "mutual participation model" and a "contractual model." Although these models have been discussed primarily in the literature of medical ethics, analogies for other professions are evident.

Szasz and Hollender have identified the mutual participation model and find it an especially appropriate one for situations where the patients are intelligent and well-educated. They bring out that the model places a value on humans, recognizes their equality, and requires specifically that professionals and those they deal with be equal in power; further, any dependency created in the relationship should be mutual, as should any satisfactions experienced.[42] Finding such a relationship to be basically a visionary, friendship relationship, Veatch advocates what he finds to be a more realistic alternative to the paternalistic model—the contractual model. This he describes as a model showing two individuals interacting, both incurring obligations and both accruing benefits. Veatch thinks this model, which is based on such societal values as freedom and recognition of the dignity of humans, circumvents the problem with the paternalistic or "priestly" tradition that ascribes decision-making to the doctor.[43]

The upshot of all of this is that even if professions have treated their clients and patients in a paternalistic fashion, this need not be the case; there are alternative models, and subscription to one of them does not rob professionals of their essence. Put differently, one has latitude to develop a conception of the professional's role that rejects any claim of paternalistic treatment of patients and clients being essential to the role.

Autonomy

Pound posits autonomy as a "presupposition" of a profession and brings this out by contrasting a member of a profession with a government servant:

> It cannot be insisted too strongly that the idea of a profession is inconsistent with performance of its function, exercise of its art, by or under the supervision of a government bureau. A profession presupposes individuals free to pursue a learned art so as to make for the highest development of human powers. The

individual servant of a government exercising under supervision of his official superiors a calling managed by a government bureau can be no substitute for the scientist, the philosopher, the teacher, each freely applying his chosen field of learning.[44]

It is noteworthy that Pound attempts to justify the presupposition by pointing to how it furthers the development of human powers. As such, the justification seems to bear on a more general claim, like Kant's in the eighteenth century, that one's development into an autonomous, moral agent is predicated on one's being free, and more recent claims that the development of personality and the full human potential rests on individual liberty.[45] It seems what would have to be explored in evaluating Pound fully is whether professionals are different from all humans in that professionals have as part of their essence the need for some freedom greater than others. If not, then Pound may have isolated merely a presupposition of humans and not of professionals. And, along these lines, one might question whether his claim about governmental restriction may not be part of a general thesis about the intrusion of government into the lives of any humans.

If Pound and others are correct that autonomy is a part of the idea of a profession, then, as one commentator brings out, they do not square with the realities of practice, and a paradox arises because of this:

> there are some indications in recent studies of a great paradox. Part of the cherished freedom of a professional worker is not merely to do his work according to his own best judgment and conscience, but also to choose his own style of work and economy of effort. Lawyers who practice alone—at least in a sample of them taken in Chicago—are the captives and chore boys of their client. They have no freedom to choose a branch of law and make themselves expert or learned in it. Most of them, in time, do find their practice narrowed to a special line of chores: they have become specialists by default.[46]

Following up on this line of reasoning, one may bring out further how the "high degree of autonomy" offered earlier as characteristic of the professional comes under suspicion as an essential feature. Consider, for example, associates of a law firm and the issue of autonomy. Consider how senior partners place expectations and restrictions on associates' activity and time, as do judges before whom they argue, the opposing counsels, and their clients, not to mention the code of professional ethics. While counterparts to these sources of restriction on autonomy may exist among nonprofessionals, it is not at all clear that they are of this great a magnitude. And even if professionals enjoy more autonomy than nonprofessionals, the sorts of restrictions placed on the professional's conduct, arguably, are sufficient to deny that any high degree of autonomy is an essential feature of the calling. Thus goes the case for the side opposing Pound's strong claim that autonomy is a presupposition of a profession.

Leadership

Leadership has been clearly identified by some to go hand in hand with a profession. Says Adams:

> Taking into account the facets of social existence we have been mentioning, we can recognize the enormous import of the concept of the professions as a cultural creation defining a type of leadership.... As a leader in the society, as a man of higher education, he [the professional] is expected to be a decisive bearer and critic of the culture.... The cultural leadership incumbent upon the professional cannot be effectively carried out without the participation of professional men in the non-profit voluntary associations that provide the opportunity for the sifting of facts about public policy, and for the achievement of tentative consensus and of implementation of that consensus through political and non-political means.[47]

In developing a notion of the "community professional," Robert Schultz combines the motif of the professional's having special obligations as a public servant with the notion that the professional should assume roles of leadership in the community. Schultz thinks these duties become clear if we attend to the historical and logical origins of professionalism and ask for the significance of these for the professional in contemporary society:

> Perhaps some preliminary illumination can be derived from turning away momentarily from talk of professional and its vocabulary to consider the origins—in both the historical and logical sense—of our moral commitment to meeting human needs. What is the image under which we go to our tasks? For many of us, I think, this is an image of a human being in need coming into contact with another human being with a special capacity for meeting such a need. And the moral dimension of the image suggests pretty clearly what ought to ensue. The skilled practitioner should size up the problem quickly and accurately, should work efficiently and unselfishly to meet the need, using as many of the available knowledge resources as possible and should emerge from the encounter strengthened in his/her human potency and freedom. And yet we all know, too, that this image of the informed, unselfish, life-enhancing service doesn't fit somehow in the "real world." Given that many of us...will find in this a recognizable description of our predicament, can we make use of the language and ideals of professionalism as giving shape to our work?... The focus of professional performance is set by an awareness of a broader context of social reality. And crucial to the vision are the "spirit" within which professional skills are applied, and a sense of moral fraternity and leadership.[48]

What about this notion that the nature of a profession demands that its members be leaders in the community? Let us consider the other side of the debate. Such a notion can be seen as resting on a dubious assumption that one highly trained in some specific area thereby has acquired or has always been in possession of the ability to lead as set out above. Professor Veatch points out how we wrongly attribute to those with some special technical competency the ability to make value judgments surrounding technical questions and has labeled this the Fallacy of the Generalization of Expertise.[49] In short, just because a surgeon, for example, has the technical know-how to perform a radical mastectomy upon discovering a malignant tumor in a patient's breast, the surgeon is not thereby competent to determine that surgical removal of the breast is better than radiation therapy if the data indicate that the two procedures are comparably successful. *A fortiori*, it would seem that we commit an even grosser fallacy if we ascribe to experts in a particular area special competence to make decisions for others in matters *unrelated* to their expertise. Moreover, if we can recognize that specialized training and the ability to lead do not necessarily go hand in hand, it would seem to do more damage than good to encourage members of a profession to think of themselves as bearing the onus of community leadership simply because they are members of a profession. For we could likely end up placing expectations of leadership upon those ill-suited to meet them.

Codes of Ethics and Professional Associations

In constructing an understanding of a profession built mainly from the blocks already mentioned, Weckstein suggests that a code of ethics is also crucial and in so doing seems to posit yet another distinct feature of the concept:

> The essence of a profession is that the measure of success is the service performed and not the gains amassed.... This emphasis upon learning and the rendition of needed services suggests two other common professional attributes: (1) the development of a code of ethics and (2) a system of internal controls to enforce these professional standards. The theory is that since the acquisition of professional skill requires a special aptitude and an extensive period of study or training, laymen are incapable of adequately performing professional services for themselves and usually unable to determine whether or not a professional person has acted properly.... Thus, a layman...must put his faith in professional certification, codes of ethics, and professional disciplinary enforcement.[50]

Adams, too, points to a code of ethics as an essential feature of a profession as he offers perhaps the longest list of significant characteristics:

> let us say that a profession includes these features: it performs a unique and essential social service; it requires a long period of general and specialized training, usually in connection with a university; it presupposes skills that are subjected to rational analysis; service to the community rather than economic gain is supposed to be a dominant motive; standards of competence are defined by a comprehensive self-governing organization or practitioner; a high degree of autonomy is presupposed for the individual practitioner and for the professional groups as a whole; some code of ethics is adumbrated by the professional group for the performance of its service.[51]

Codes and the attendant enforcement used to insure for the laity professional conduct by members of a profession may not, according to one commentator, be the most significant factor in controlling professional behavior; internal controls, we find, are operative. Says Moore:

> Without review and enforcement mechanisms, professional codes may be little more than window dressing, perhaps more designed to give false comfort to the laity than to guide the practitioner. Yet it is also important to stress the efficacy of informal controls. The physician in group practice or in the hospital setting, the attorney in the law firm, the Army officer, the university professor work in situations in which other experts are working, or may do so at virtually any time.[52]

We might see such observations as a challenge to the claim that codes are essential features of professions. If, in fact, they are mere window dressing, then, even if all professions have them, their relevance to developing a conception of a profession is only apparent. Moreover, that professionals work in a context in which they and their co-workers, in effect, keep each other in line, may be seen as a phenomenon of any work setting. It is not at all clear from Moore's statement that professions value the use of internal controls that he intends to suggest only professions do so. So even if, in this line of reasoning, internal controls and not codes are primarily operative, we still have identified nothing peculiar to the profession.

Turning to professional associations, we find Carr-Saunders portraying as an invariable historical occurrence that, whenever there are professions, there are professional associations:

> The history of the evolution of the professions brings a significant fact to light. As soon as a profession emerges, the practitioners are moved by the recognition of common interests to attempt to form a professional association.[53]

He goes on to identify the motives professionals may have for doing so, pointing to guaranteeing exclusive patronage, maintaining competency, and insuring professional conduct:

> They do indeed aim at obtaining for their members the exclusive patronage of clients and employers requiring the service of their craft. But with this aim is associated the ideal of including within their ranks all competent practitioners. The qualified members of a profession are thus moved to form associations and mutually to guarantee their own competence. But this is not the only motive leading to association. Another motive is present from the beginning.... The responsible members of a profession in fact desire to see a proper standard of professional conduct set up and maintained.... Thus professional associations define and enforce rules of professional conduct.[54]

A sustained evaluation of the importance of professional associations in understanding professions is contained in our next section dealing with law as a profession. So let us now temporarily suspend our evaluation of professional associations and take stock in what we have done.

SUMMARY

To this point we have examined a variety of views detailing the features of a profession. We endeavored to show what controversy surrounded these features to allow the reader to evaluate critically which of them seem to be the most likely for constructing a viable understanding of what a profession is or a conception of one's role as a professional. This discussion would obviously have most significance for professionals who are to construct conceptions of themselves as professionals to guide their conduct. This discussion also has considerable relevance for anyone who wishes to participate in the dialogue about how best to conceive of professionals in order to influence professionals in how they choose to see themselves. And this discussion has general relevance for everyone in that it gives all of us as role constructors a sense of the range of variables that can bear on one's constructing a role and how a case for and against these being included in one's construction can reasonably be made. It assists all of us in breaking out of our nonreflective and partially reflective attitudes that often obstruct us in thinking about our roles, for it helps us to see the genuine issues surrounding the elements for constructing a role and the importance of our adopting a critical attitude to resolve these issues and to build our conceptions from our resolutions of these issues.

We saw put forth as essential for an understanding of a profession that its members have special responsibilities and obligations to the public, that their labor is to be done in the spirit of public service, that they are to provide leadership for the community, that they have acquired special skills and knowledge for entry, that they have organized supervision of their activities, that they are guided by codes of ethics, and that they are autonomous. Now, it does seem that each of the features has some *prima facie* plausibility as a candidate for being adopted as an essential feature of a profession. Assuming this to be the case, can we say anything systematic about the predicates under consideration that might throw some further light on one's developing an understanding of what a profession is?

Arguably, all of the features we have dealt with point to reasons for thinking that the work of the group is qualitatively better or nobler than other types of work, and, as such, may be seen as grounds for respect for the group. As confirmation, one might turn to the attempts of various work groups that traditionally have not been seen as professions to secure that designation presumably because of the special status and respect thereby conferred.

If there is some sense to saying that these characteristics of a profession may be seen as grounds for respect, then a factor involved in adopting this as a feature of a profession, I wish to bring out, is public perception. Let us consider this claim more closely. Whether something is worthy of respect, it seems, cannot strictly be a function of some finite set of grounds for respect. For it always seems intelligible to question whether or deny that something claimed to be worthy of respect really is so, even after all of the grounds for the attribution of this quality have been cited. One's response to a variety of factors cited as grounds for recognizing something as worthy of respect seems crucial to one's assenting to that entity's being worthy of respect. Thus, should it be suggested to a Marxist that John Dough is worthy of respect because Mr. Dough moved from rags to riches by founding his own company for the production of good, five-dollar cigars, because he is an elder of his church, and because he has toed the Republican line for the past thirty years, it is more likely than not that the recitation of such factors will evoke contempt, not respect, in the Marxist. Other qualities seem to function in this manner in that their proper attribution seems to involve, in part, a consideration of how some perceiver reacts to some situation or to pieces of information presented to the perceiver. Thus, one may attempt to create a horrifying movie and build into it ingredients traditionally thought to elicit horror from the audience, but whether the movie is horrifying and whether we can properly call it a horror movie, requires our investigating the audience's responses. In like fashion, I suggest, the determination of whether something is worthy of respect hinges, in part, on whether it is, in fact, perceived to be such upon the recitation of the grounds for respect.

Let us apply this insight to our concern about constructing a conception of a profession. If one sees that all the candidates we turned to in delineating a profession may be summed up as grounds for respect for the occupation, one may adopt worthiness of respect as an additional feature of what a profession is. But, in the final analysis, whether this feature can be legitimately included in a viable construction of what a profession is is a function of public perception. As we now turn to law as a profession, we will consider, in part, the public's perception of this working group's meriting respect along with the extent to which law displays the features commonly associated with professions. But first, let us consider some of the peculiarities of law. As we do so, we begin to see illustrated the task of our harmonizing our constructed roles and their related rules. Here, of course, the roles that come into play are those of the professional and of the lawyer. Lawyers occupy both roles and must develop not merely a conception of each but a consistent profile of the lawyer as professional. Again, we can see this specific problem which the lawyer faces as illustrative of one we all face as we square how we have conceived of our humanity with the specific roles which we occupy.

LAW AS A PROFESSION

In drawing out some of the distinctive features of the profession of law, some analysts have compared it to other professions. Just as other professions can be seen as having a primary goal—the medical profession, for example, has as its goal health or, more specifically, the prolongation of life and the relief of pain and suffering—the legal profession, too, has a primary goal, namely, justice. But in contrast with other professions, the law often deals with problems more closely tied to the economic status of the client. Thus, when lawyers specialize, they tend to deal with a particular economic class; the problems associated with workman's compensation claims, for example, belong to a different economic class of people, in general, than the problems associated with, say, corporate securities.[55] Medical and spiritual problems, in contrast, do not seem to vary in this way as one moves from one economic class to another. One might also observe from the comparative perspective a discontinuity between what occurs at legal as against medical clinics. The types of problems presented to the staff of the legal-aid clinic are few compared with the broad spectrum of those at the medical clinic.[56]

If the specialized practice of law is restricted to some particular economic class, the practice generally is also restricted to political boundaries, unlike in other professions.[57] There is a sense, however, in which the particular skills of lawyers allow them to broaden the scope of their activity in a way that the skills of other professionals do not. Referred to here is the ability of lawyers to step naturally into the political arena. Skills of the lawyer, like those of compromise, debate, and law-making, are congruent with those needed in politics.[58]

Other commentators, in discussing what is peculiar to the legal profession, turn to the particular qualities required of the professional qua attorney. One list includes industry, legal learning, broad culture, strong will, oratorical power, moral courage, and human insight or sympathy. Such were distilled by Grafton Rogers in his "The Armament of Lawyers" from his tabulation of positive qualities displayed by lawyers in a survey of 160 biographies of lawyers.[59] And such are pointed to as indicators of success in the profession.[60] Discrimination, character, industry, scholarship, courage, and a sense of social responsibility were the qualities most frequently listed in a 1935 survey of alumni of Illinois Law.[61] Considering these catalogs of qualities, Drinker suggests that some of the most important qualities went unmentioned, including "imagination or wisdom and common sense."[62] And "unwearied assiduity" is pointed to as a quality requisite for entry into the profession, given the devotion required to master the range of legal knowledge.[63]

To this point, none of what has been said about the particular nature of the legal profession reflects any sustained effort to illustrate how the legal profession displays some of the features we considered of any profession. But, as a matter of fact, many of the features we found identified as central to a profession have received special attention in discussions about the peculiarities of law as a profession, and it is to these discussions that we can now turn. Here especially we see an opportunity to observe how one's construction of one's roles as professional and as attorney requires a reconciling, harmonizing, or integrating of the features one chooses to build into these conceptions or of the rules that attend these conceptions. Drinker offers a historical account of how public service came to be tied to the profession of law:

> This tradition of public service, with the remuneration an incident, originated long ago with our legal ancestors, the barristers, in their Inns of Court. They were originally almost exclusively men of substantial origins, often younger sons of England's leading families, who for the most part were not dependent on their profession for their livelihood. As was common in that age, they looked down on "trade" and particularly on its spirit of competition and *caveat emptor*. The young men who went from Boston, New York, Philadelphia, and the South to study at the Inns of Court and who on their return became the leaders at the bar here, brought with them these traditions, which despite the urge of "business" have been preserved and formulated by our bar association.[64]

Marks considers the attitude of the contemporary public interest lawyer and finds the spirit of public service still alive:

> "I want to be a lawyer, not a public interest lawyer, just a lawyer. I would be perfectly willing to see 'public interest law' pass from compensatory effort incorporated into the day-to-day workings of the legal profession." In this way the public interest lawyer is reminding the profession of the true meaning of service ahead of gain. It is here that present experience may tutor the profession as a whole.[65]

Regardless of the extent to which public service may be part of the true nature of the profession, Marks observes that this requirement is by no means met, in fact, by all lawyers and suggests that older lawyers and firm managers are the chief violators of this expectation of public service:

> The life styles of public interest lawyers and the managers of
> firms are apt to be different, and these differences turn on
> sought-for levels of economic and social comfort. They indi-
> rectly affect the definition of professional role—principally
> through the mechanism of client selection or rejection. Clients
> selected by the firm are those who represent the interests that
> make the partners comfortable or enable them to attain the
> standard of living they want to have or have to have. Whatever
> they may say about professional duty to all comers, the older
> lawyers' choices of public interest clients are misdirected by the
> life styles of those lawyers,...the fact remains that the profes-
> sional ethic that dominates the private law firm relegates all but
> a few of the new breed lawyers to an avocational pursuit of pro-
> fessional responsibilities as they see it.[66]

In further exploring how the service orientation of professions
may become weakened, Pound draws our attention to professional
associations and in so doing brings into focus another general element of professions. Pound's undertaking, sponsored by the American Bar Association, represents a sustained apology for bar associations and their significance for the life of the profession of law.
Pound's primary argument draws our attention to a lesson we can
learn from history. As such, it may be seen as representing in itself a
contribution to our understanding what a profession is, given our
analysis of how something's history may contribute to our understanding of it.

The period of history in question Pound dubs "the era of decadence." During this time, 1836–1870, bar associations disbanded,
requirements for admission to the bar were severely weakened, and
consequent to these developments was the deprofessionalization of
law. Bar associations, Pound argues, are needed to ensure the service orientation of law, for they are the vehicles for the delivery of
this service. So associations become essential to the profession of
law through their connection with its service orientation. Pound then
suggests that the solution to the problem of the era of decadence was
the organization of the profession and that "completion and perfec-

tion of professional organization is what may save us from another era of decadence and resulting injury to law and to constitutional democracy."[67] Thus, the need for bar associations.

More concretely, Pound tells us that, during this era, public criticism mounted concerning the restrictions imposed by an organized bar on the practice of law. The result was that between 1842 and 1851 the states of New Hampshire, Maine, Wisconsin, and Indiana enacted legislation that in effect substituted a state residency or citizenship requirement for an educational requirement for entry to the bar.[68] If we understand a profession, as did Pound, as "an organized body of men pursuing a learned art in the spirit of a public service," we can recognize that, during this era of decadence, not only did the aspect of law's being a learned art disappear but also its public service aspect:

> The era of emergent democracy, in its leveling zeal, and the succeeding era of the beginning of the frontier, in its faith in the ability of any man to do anything and its zeal for unrestrained individual freedom, sought to substitute for the profession pursuing a learned art, an uneducated, untrained trade pursuing a money-making calling in the spirit of a business.[69]

In detailing his view on the significance of the bar for the maintenance of the integrity of the profession and for the preservation of that element—service—that makes it a profession, Pound continues:

> The bar association...is an essential element of professional life. It is only through organization that the spirit of public service can be developed and maintained and crucial types of public service can be rendered effectively. It is the bar association, not the individual lawyer, that can maintain high educational standards insuring a learned profession, that can maintain high standards of character or a pre-requisite of admission to practice that can formulate and maintain high standards of ethical conduct in relations both with client and with court. The public has a deep interest in having a well organized bar as

part of the machinery of administering justice in a complex social and economic order.[70]

In evaluating Pound's views, we have reason, at the outset, to consider these claims guardedly, given that Pound's conclusion makes necessary the existence of a professional bar association and that the study was sponsored by the American Bar Association. Looking critically at the claims on their merits confirms that Pound has overstated his case. Organization, we are told, is the only way to promote public service and maintain high standards of education and character for admission. We are led to believe that the alternatives are organization through a private bar association or no organization and reversion to an era of decadence. Unexplored here are alternatives like maintaining such standards through an organization of government or placing nonlawyers in charge of such an organization. It is not clear what control by a bar association can achieve that control by some other group or agency cannot. It seems that essential to what Pound is arguing is that there must be some set of controls on members of the profession if elements considered important in identifying them as professionals—education and service—are to be maintained. While Pound, strictly speaking, only establishes the need for *some* form of agency to preserve and promote the legal profession, he may be right, practically, about the form this agency would take—presumably a bar association run primarily by and for lawyers. Coming into play in this assessment is Drinker's observation above about the motives professionals may have for forming a professional association—motives of controlling patronage, competency, and conduct. Taking these motives into account, along with other qualities of self-direction and autonomy considered above, we can infer that such a group of workers would resist externally imposed standards. Putting together our modification of Pound's thesis about the necessity of professional associations with Drinker's view about why we can expect to find professional associations where there are professions, we get, upon analysis, a fuller picture of professional associations to guide the role constructor.

Let us now consider the debate over whether the legal profession displays the quality of being worthy of respect. The question is particularly interesting against the backdrop of well-known expressions by the public of dissatisfaction. Recognizing that such dissatisfaction occurs with any system of law, Pound isolates four causes:

> Inevitable...mechanical operation of rules and so of laws; the inevitable difference in rate of progress between law and public opinion; a general popular assent that the administration of justice is an easy task to which anyone is competent; and, last but not least, inborn human impatience of restraint.... In pioneer frontier America the third and fourth had serious effects upon law and lawyers.[71]

Drinker attributes complaints about lawyers to the public's being uninformed, yet he points to evidence suggesting that most responsible people hold lawyers in high esteem.[72] He draws attention to the fact that the American and British peoples have placed lawyers in public positions of trust, have done so for five hundred years, and have drawn on these professionals to fill such positions more than on any other group.[73] The fact that lawyers are called upon to hold office, however, may have less to do with their being held in high esteem than with the vital service they render. The nature of this vital service, on Pound's account, is the preservation of the democratic way of life. He reasons that, to the extent that law impedes autocratic rule, lawyers preserve democracy, and therein lies the service the citizenry turns to them for:

> Law and hence lawyers are the enemies of autocracy. In consequence, American states, as constitutional democracies, are characteristically legal polities in which the constitution is the "supreme law of the land,"... Under our polity many political questions are as well legal and many legal questions are also political. Thus our constitutional polity is so legal as to be dependent upon lawyers for interpretation, application, and maintenance against official absolution and legal encroach-

ment. More than any other people, the American people, more than any other society in history, American politically organized society, a democratic society constitutionally and federally organized, relies upon law and so upon lawyers.[74]

Another commentator working with the nature of the vital service provided points to the relationship between the number of lawyers in the society and the amount of liberty, claiming that that relationship is one of direct proportion.[75]

Let us pursue further this dispute over whether attorneys are worthy of respect. On the one hand, we find expressions of discontent over "legalese" or lawyer jargon and over such phenomena as open-ended fee agreements between lawyers and clients.[76] Some allege that lawyer advertising is the source of diminished respect for the attorney in that the practice ultimately underscores the commercial and obscures the service orientation of the attorney.[77] Moreover, it is alleged that attorneys can and do, at their clients' behests, bring unjust or groundless suits designed merely to harass.[78]

On the other hand, countervailing considerations do weigh against some of these criticisms. Surely no one would criticize the surgeon for using, in the operating room, specialized language that had no significance to the mind untrained in medicine. Moreover, the Supreme Court has recognized that previous restrictions on lawyer advertising "may be seen to reflect the profession's failure to reach out and serve the community" and that it is anachronistic to think that lawyers, once thought of in Great Britain as practicing to serve rather than to earn a living, are above trade.[79] Also, it has been argued that attorneys are not morally blameworthy for acts like bringing a suit to harass; there is a wrong involved, but it is inherent in the legal system that permits such an action and not one attributable to those who perform such actions.[80]

So, we would be wrong to assume attorneys are not respected simply because they are sometimes targets of disparaging remarks; reasonable responses to these remarks are readily available. Further, there is no contradiction in saying, on the one hand, that certain activities of attorneys are criticizable and even deserving of condemnation, and, on the other, that attorneys, nevertheless, are worthy of respect; even in the face of disrespect for particular attorneys, there may be respect for the legal profession. But again, as brought out above, one's inclusion of this feature in one's construction should hinge on empirical concerns—whether attorneys are actually perceived as worthy of respect. Here we have made a few comments that are probative of the matter.

SUMMARY

With this consideration of the ways in which law displays some of the qualities commonly turned to in identifying the nature of a profession, let us now place all of this in perspective. While we have preferred no single, new understanding of what a profession is, our discussion should not thereby seem wanting. For we adopted a method that rejects the usual approach in the literature on the professions. Unlike the other approaches, which analyze what the features of a profession are and then deliver the resulting wisdom to the reader for adoption, our method respects the reader as a role constructor employing a critical attitude. What we recognized we could do to assist the professional and the lawyer as professional in the endeavor of self-construction was to provide the raw materials for this construction, and we did this not simply by surveying features that have been identified as essential to a profession but by providing some critical commentary in the spirit of allowing the reader to perceive that issues and controversies can and do surround these features. While it is evidently beyond the scope of this work to provide similar analyses for all roles, it is reasonable to see our contribution to thinking about the professional role as relevant to the construction of any role. As we brought out, the constructor of any role can glean from our discussion of the professional role something about the number of variables that can enter one's deliberations about a role, the extent to which people can reasonably differ about the inclusion of these factors, how the constructed role structures one's conduct with rules, and the plausibility of individuals who occupy these roles making the decisions about how best to conceive them. Of course, what has been assumed throughout is the body of theory that we developed in chapter 2 to make intelligible these notions of one's constructing a particular notion of the self and then acting in accord with this conception or with rules consonant with it.

To explore further the implications of this theory for the attorney, it is first worth observing that a number of the variables we have isolated for constructing a conception of an attorney are context-bound; they refer us not just to the adversary environs within which attorneys practice but also to the more general political environments of the society. Consider, for example, Pound's discussion of the autonomous character of lawyers and his view of the relationship between that feature of attorneys and their society. Consider also how, in discussing the issue of respect for attorneys, we expressed concern over the possibility in an adversary system of their bringing suits merely to harass others. A complete conception of an attorney then would include a clear reference to the environment in which this attorney operates. As we shall see in the next chapter, a single conception of these environments does not come ready-made, but it too must be constructed from the variables. And again, in watching how attorneys can build conceptions of themselves by considering how to think about their environments, we have before us a model for general ethics of how people, in constructing conceptions of themselves and their roles, must consider how they are to conceive of their environments.

MELONI, Gino. *Lotta dei Galli* (*Cocks Fighting*). 1953. Oil, 32 x 24".
E. Hintermann Collection, Milan.

4
▼

The Attorney's Environments
Adversary and Socio-political Systems

That attorneys should not reveal the confidences of their clients, that they should preserve the independence of their judgment by avoiding such things as representing clients with conflicting interests, and that they should provide zealous representation for their clients are, at one and the same time, some of the major responsibilities of attorneys and the source of some of the best known and most intractable ethical problems for lawyers. Of the sixteen basic rules of the American Bar Association's *Model Rules of Professional Conduct* that set out the most fundamental obligations of attorneys in the client-lawyer relationship, five pertain to these areas. Of the nine basic canons of the American Bar Association's *Model Code of Professional Responsibility,* one is devoted to each of these three areas. And commonly known is the sort of ethical problems associated with them: May attorneys breach confidences to prevent perjury or some other crime being committed by their clients? Should they, in the name of zealous representation, humiliate and attempt to discredit adverse witnesses who they know to be truthful? What should they do if a conflict of interest arises during the course of representation, say, in a divorce settlement where what initially appeared to be an amicable parting and one conducive to a lawyer's representing both parties develops into a confrontation of hostile and polarized parties? It takes but a moment's reflection to realize that these obligations and dilemmas are rooted in a system for the administration of justice where partisan advocates on each of two sides of a dispute have the responsibility for presenting their cases in the best possible light to a neutral judge or jury that decides the case on the basis of these presentations. This system, of course, is the adversary system of justice. Surely the ground for keeping confidential the secrets of the client is that their revelation may help the other side and harm one's own. And the win-lose nature of the preceding suggests that lawyers should represent their clients with zeal much as competing teams would pursue victory in the sports arena. And would not the chances of winning be impaired were conflicting interests to weigh on the attorney's judgement?

The trouble with the characterization above is that it leads us to believe that, while we can appreciate how ethical issues important for the attorney originate in, and take their complexion from, the adversary environment, our main task is to focus on the issues themselves. We are led to believe that the adversary system exists as a fixed and given environment ready for us to take note of. It is a primary thesis of this chapter that far more attention must first be devoted to a study of the adversary environment, given that there is, in fact, no single conception of this system, that there are, accordingly, opportunities for one's constructing a conception of an adversary system, and that, depending on how one constructs this conception, one will find the particular ethical problems shaped differently. Put another way, just as attorneys must consider reflectively and piece together conceptions of themselves as professionals, as attorneys, and as humans, so too must they consider reflectively and piece together conceptions of an important aspect of the environment of attorneys, the system of justice within which they operate; for part of how they understand themselves is how they conceive of their environs. Thus, just as the constructed conceptions of their roles advised on how attorneys ought to act, so too do their constructions of the adversary environment.

A similar point is developed as regards the socio-political environment of attorneys which we likewise depict as open for a construction that advises on how attorneys should act. We will undertake a fuller development of this claim after first attending to the more immediate and perhaps more directly relevant aspect of the attorney's environment—its adversarial nature.

In what follows, we will consider conceptions of the adversary system, where zealous advocacy is the key issue; its justifications, where its bringing out the truth is the main issue; and criticisms of it, many of which focus on the clash between zealous advocacy and truth. Although this structuring of the material is common, it departs from the usual impression conveyed of there being a single phenomenon to investigate. Even writers who hint at some diversity end up positing a uniform view. Says one, "The Adversary process should not be viewed as a single technique or collection of techniques; it is a unified concept that works by use of a number of interconnecting procedures."[1] Another, who draws our attention to some "other interpretations of the adversary system,"[2] nonetheless suggests with such language that there is some basic system that lends itself to interpretation.

During the course of our investigation, we will see how some justifications are irrelevant to some conceptions, how some criticisms are reasonably directed only at certain conceptions, and how all of these considerations of conceptions, justifications, and criticisms are relevant for the attorney's construction of an adversarial environment. For example, if the adversary system is primarily conceived as a dispute-settling mechanism with the ascertainment of truth figuring low as a feature of its design or purpose, a justification of such a system for the administration of justice that highlights its abilities to adduce the truth is little to the point, and any criticism of such a system's being faulty for failing to procure the truth is, in a sense, wide of the mark. As such considerations become more apparent in what follows, the need for attorneys to place some order on the multiplicity of ways of conceiving of an adversary system becomes more urgent. Once again, our considering the attorney's construction, this time of an adversarial environment, illustrates for the general reader the task each of us faces of thinking critically about and building conceptions of our environments.

CONCEPTIONS OF AN ADVERSARY SYSTEM: THE BASIC SETTING

A useful but not rigid means of classifying elements commonly employed to define the adversary system is to consider first the features of the basic setting, then of its operation, and then of its broader context. As for the first, let us attend to a description of the parties, the decision maker, and the forensic and public nature of the context. Primarily at issue here is how active the decision maker is, with one's view on that matter affecting how one conceives of party participation.

In speaking of adjudication generally, and as a way of showing that the adversary system embraces the essentials of adjudication, Fuller identifies party participation as "an essential condition for the functioning of adjudication."[3] More specifically, he tells us that "the distinguishing characteristic of adjudication lies in the fact that it confers on the affected party a peculiar form of participation in the decision, that of presenting proofs and reasoned arguments for a decision in his favor."[4] With party participation so described, we see going hand in hand with it the notion of an impartial judge: "If...we start with the notion of a process of decision in which the affected party's participation consists in an opportunity to present proofs and reasoned arguments, the office of judge or arbitrator and the requirement of impartiality follow as necessary conditions."[5] So, focusing on the idea of adjudication itself and its affinity to party participation, Fuller is able to bring to the fore the elements of there being interested parties, their being in a setting where, through rational argumentation, they are allowed to urge the validity of their causes, and there being an impartial arbiter. In another work, Fuller identifies these elements as being necessary ingredients of the philosophy of the adversary system that stresses a separation of functions: "The philosophy of adjudication that is expressed in 'the adversary system' is, speaking generally, a philosophy that insists on keeping distinct the function of the advocate, on the one hand, from that of the judge, or of the judge from that of the jury, on the other. The decision of the case is for the judge or for the judge and jury. That decision must be as objective and as free from bias as it possibly can."[6]

In concurrence with the elements of Fuller's account, Landsman brings out how they basically describe the adversary system since the earliest days of the American nation and adds the attribute of passivity to the description of the decision maker: "Since at least the time of the American Revolution, courts in the United States have employed a system of procedure that depends upon a neutral and passive fact finder (either judge or jury) to resolve disputes on the basis of information provided by contending parties during formal proceedings."[7] And where Fuller introduced the notion of the impartial arbiter through the idea of party participation, Landsman proceeds in the other direction, making clear how the passivity of the fact finder requires activity on the part of the parties: "Intimately connected with the requirements of decision-maker passivity and neutrality is the procedural principle that the parties are responsible for producing all the evidence upon which the decision will be based."[8] Also included in Landsman's account of the rudimentary features of the adversary system which we do not find in Fuller's are sets of rules—procedural, evidentiary, and ethical—that structure the forensic setting.[9]

In contrast to Landsman's introduction of, and reliance on, passivity in deriving the elements of the adversary system is the longstanding common-law rule permitting judges to examine and call witnesses. Says McCormick in his *Handbook of the Law of Evidence*, "Under the Anglo-American adversary trial system, the parties and their counsel have the primary responsibility for finding, selecting, and presenting the evidence. However, our system of party-investigation and party-presentation has some limitations. It is a means to the end of disclosing truth and administering justice; and for reaching this end the judge may exercise various powers. Prominent among these powers is his power to call and examine witnesses. The judge in his discretion may examine any witness to bring out needed facts which have not been elicited by the parties."[10] Further, not only may judges be active with regard to their general power to question witnesses. They may put questions in a fashion generally unavailable to counsel—by asking leading questions—and, moreover, they may comment on the evidence.

Now, in most states, such commenting is not permitted, and this prohibition has implications for the judge's asking leading questions, since they may amount to implied comment on the evidence; the idea is that the answer to the leading question may seem to be endorsed by the judge as true and, thus, in effect the judge has commented on the evidence.[11] Further, even where the common-law power of judges to comment is retained—in a few states, in the federal courts, and in all jurisdictions in cases tried before the bench or with a judge only and no jury—and even when judges' powers to examine are virtually without restriction, McCormick admonishes that judges must be on their guard not to step out of their role of judges: "...the judge, though he has a wide power to examine witnesses, must avoid extreme exercises of the power to question, just as he must avoid extreme exercises of the power to comment. He must not assume the role of an advocate or of a prosecutor. If his questions are too partisan or even if they are too extensive, he faces the risk that the appellate court will find that he has crossed the line between judging and advocacy."[12] So, as we see restrictions and warnings issuing to judges as they enter active roles, we begin to get a sense of the controversy surrounding an active arbiter in an adversary set-up.

As mentioned earlier, another fashion in which judges step out of the passive role which some assigned to them above is when they exercise their power to call witnesses. Common situations where judges do so, says McCormick, include those where judges call impartial, expert witness of their own choosing; this usually occurs when the testimony of partisan experts seems to be reaching an impasse and when it appears that the prosecution is unwilling to call a necessary witness because it fears that the witness may be hostile;

according to the rules governing cross-examination, it is forbidden to impeach one's own witness. Either side may discredit or impeach a witness called by the judge.[13]

From these considerations, it is evident that debatable in conceiving of an adversary system is the extent to which party presentation precludes active participation by the judge. Another way of striking the issue is in terms of judicial passivity being associated with adversary systems of justice and activity with inquisitorial systems. In describing the adversary system as a "procedure for trial," Hazard identifies as its "essential feature" that "a decision is made by a judge, or judge with jury, who finds the facts and determines the law from submissions made by partisan advocates on behalf of the parties."[14] In comparing the adversary system so described with the essential feature of the inquisitorial system of countries following the civil law tradition, such as France and Germany, we find the activity of the judge central in striking the distinction: "In this system of trial,...the judge determines the law and finds the facts by his own active investigation and inquiries at trial."[15] So, we might read the focus on the passivity of the judge in the descriptions of the adversary system as a means of keeping distinct one system of justice from another, as Hazard has explicitly done here, while at the same time taking note of the judicial activity in adversary settings. Indeed, Hazard himself acknowledges the lack of fixity in the conception, asserting that "there is probably no 'pure' form of either system";[16] for him, though, the variability seems to enter at the level of party rather than judicial participation. More specifically, as we diminish the significance of the advocate's responsibility to develop the proofs, we can identify one variant where counsel becomes a coach to facilitate participation by the client, and another where, because the idea of securing truth is so remote, the trial becomes more of a ritual.[17]

Another theorist who focuses on the actions of the decision maker to distinguish adversary and inquisitorial systems is Belliotti. He brings out how, in the adversary system, jurors are passive observers without any right to question the witnesses and how it is each party that calls its own witnesses and presents its evidence.

This is in contradistinction to the inquisitorial system, according to Belliotti, where "evidence is gathered by an official inquiry presided over by a judge."[18]

It is often in the context of comparing adversarial and inquisitorial systems that the forensic nature of the adversary setting is elucidated. And this is usually developed in accord with the respective systems' commitments to arriving at the truth. As opposed to the inquisitorial system, the adversary system, with its two parties, two advocates, and arbiter, provides, says Freedman, a form "of organized and institutionalized confrontation leading to varieties of the truth rather than to the revelation of absolute truth."[19] Such elements imply a competition of advocates. Underlining this competition as the difference, Belliotti points out that, unlike the adversary system, the judicial process in the inquisitorial system is seen as "the state's necessary response to the alleged commission of a crime" with the tribunal's ascertaining objective truth being to the interest of everyone.[20]

As will be developed more fully when we turn to justifications of the adversary system, some justify it in terms of the system's being the best for arriving at the truth. In such justifications, we can see how different is the conception of the system from that just adumbrated—where the pursuit of truth and the forensic nature of the adversary setting were essentially contrasted with the inquisitorial. We might here at least observe, at this early point of striving to understand the variables in the adversary setting, how some writers find much hinging on just this variable of the system's commitment. Some, Patterson and Cheatham, for example, agree with the above approaches' claim that the adversary system is not primarily in pursuit of objective truth: "The factor which distinguished and has shaped the common law trial is its adversary nature. The adversary trial gives the parties, or rather their lawyers, the primary responsibility for the proceedings.... Consequently, as is generally recognized, the common law trial is not, and was never developed to be, a scientific investigation for truth."[21] With this as a starting point, they go on to identify the basic standards governing the lawyer's conduct regarding "loyalty to the client," "candor to the court," and "fairness to his opponent."[22] "The interrelatedness of these standards is best seen when they are correlated with three basic characteristics of the trial which give rise to them: its adversary nature, its concern with resolving disputes based on past events, and its highly structured setting."[23] We are led to believe that the standards and duties of lawyers would be quite otherwise were they working in a system whose commitment to producing the truth was also otherwise. So, alternatives for thinking about the basic setting of an adversary system hinge on the significance one attaches to truth and on conceptions of how to attain it as much as they hinge on the activity of the judge and the scope of party participation.

CONCEPTIONS OF AN ADVERSARY SYSTEM: ITS OPERATION

Turning to the operation of the adversary approach, we find that figuring large in most descriptions is the zealous representation that the lawyer provides the client. While we will be focusing primarily on the different ways of thinking about such representation and what they entail, we should first take note of some descriptions of an adversary set-up where neither the language of zeal is employed nor does the concept seem essentially to be captured. Freedman, for example, after noting the elements of the adversary system—two parties, two advocates, and an arbiter—pointed out that this system assumes competency of the advocates: "Implicit in the system, if it is to be effective (and by effective I mean fair as well as functional), is that each advocate be competent—that is, able to present her side of the controversy to the arbiter in the best light."[24] This alone seems to entail nothing of zeal. One might well believe that, if we are to consider an argument for a position, whether legal or philosophical or medical, we should consider it in its strongest form and do similarly with regard to the contrary position. What we are interested in achieving is a particular outcome—the best argument—and whether that is produced by activity that can be characterized as zealous, assiduous, sober, or somber along the way, again, seems quite independent of one's having effected the strongest argument in a competent fashion. Such considerations seem more a matter of style than of necessary aspects of competent work. Now, it may be the case that, in general, the work pursued with zeal is the more likely to deliver up the best argument. But if this is the claim, it needs to be made explicit and established. The main point here is that some have emphasized that advocates are to perform in an adversary system competently, and, in emphasizing competence, depart in a plausible fashion from the usual emphasis on zealous representation.

This idea of competent representation is echoed in the thought of Marks as he describes his version of the theory of the adversary system and the responsibilities of the lawyer attendant upon so conceiving of it. "He is simply an advocate. Accordingly, he does not relate his conduct to the social rules produced by the cases he handles. He is interested solely in seeing to it that the interest of the party he represents is as ably advanced as is humanly and professionally possible."[25] Marks goes on to bring out that in the traditional view the result will be "acceptable and just" if this competent representation is rendered on each side.[26] And here he ties the conception to the responsibility: "In particular, the justness of result has been seen as absolutely dependent on the lawyer's single-minded representation of his client. The lawyer in this way has accepted responsibility for the process only, not the result."[27]

Kutak aligns closely the essence of an adversary system of justice with a competition of parties and, as he brings in competence, also does so with no reference to zeal. "Our legal system," he says, "is not cooperative but competitive, or adversarial."[28] Kutak then explains how the law governing disclosure of information in such a system illustrates a basic principle of competition theory, "that competing individuals have no legal responsibility for the competence of their counterparts on the other side of the transaction and, consequently, have no obligation to share the benefits of their own competition with the other side."[29] He goes on to bring out how, in a context of basic honesty among the parties, parties generally have no obligation to disclose information to others but do have obligations to be truthful in answers given or regarding information that is volunteered.

The American Bar Association's *Model Rules of Professional Conduct* and its *Model Code of Professional Responsibility* require not just competence of attorneys in their representation of their clients but also zeal. Canon Seven of that Code requires that the attorney "represent his client zealously within the bounds of the law" and Ethical Consideration 7-19 brings out more particularly that "the duty of a lawyer to his client and his duty to the legal system are the same: to represent his client zealously within the bounds of the law." The *Model Rules* seem to soften this exhortation to zeal in rule 1.3, which requires that "a lawyer shall act with reasonable diligence and promptness in representing a client," while noting under the "comment" after the rule, which is offered as a "guide to interpretation," that "a lawyer should act with commitment and dedication to the interests of the client and with zeal in advocacy. However, a lawyer is not bound to press for every advantage that might be realized for a client."[30] Further, the *Model Rules* are silent on the connection that we find in the *Code* between competency and zealous advocacy.

A publication of the Maryland Center for Philosophy and Public Affairs asserts that lawyers representing their clients in a zealous fashion display a training in the "Lombardi-Hays philosophy of competition." This training entails their being "steeped in it in law school and held to its standards by their codes of professional obligation. For the cornerstone of the adversary system is the lawyer's duty of zealous partisanship on behalf of his client.... the best team will be the team that wins the most."[31] Says Judge Marvin Frankel about the current adversary set-up, "The business of the advocate, simply stated, is to win if possible without violating the law."[32]

Lieberman makes reference to Lord Brougham's famous characterization of the extremes to which attorneys may go in furthering the interests of their clients and observes how such a view has endured. Says Lieberman, "Brougham's point, which succeeding generations of the bar have accepted, is that duty to client is paramount, no matter what the consequences for others, even though the entire nation may become embroiled in bitter controversy and the government weakened."[33] Brougham himself put it this way:

> An advocate, in the discharge of his duty, knows but one person in all the world, and that one person is his client. To save that client by all means and expedients, and at all hazards and costs to other persons, and among them, to himself, is his first and only duty; and in performing this duty he must not regard the alarm, the torments, the destruction which he may bring upon others. Separating the duty of the patriot from that of an advocate, he must go on reckless of consequences, though it should be his unhappy fate to involve his country in confusion.[34]

Further possibilities for thinking about the operation of an adversary system through the feature of attorneys zealously representing their clients can be had by looking at proposals for limiting zealous advocacy. Obviously Brougham recognized virtually none. Goldman brings out that lawyers' own moral views are not to impose any limitations on their advocating with zeal: "It is an accepted dogma within the legal profession, as reflected in the Code of Professional Responsibility of the American Bar Association, that a lawyer should pursue his client's interests as vigorously as possible within the bounds of the law. This means that he should not interpose his own moral opinion of those objectives of his client that are legal."[35] Landsman speaks of the profession's ethical rules as serving to control the zeal of counsel: "Since the rough-and-tumble of adversary proceedings exacerbates the natural tendency of advocates to seek to win by any means available, the adversary system employs rules of ethics to control the behavior of counsel."[36] He goes on to cite some of the specific restrictions placed on council, including one proscribing intimidation or harassment of witnesses and one restricting practices intended to mislead the trier.[37] Fuller casts the restriction on zeal in general terms, bringing out that zealous actions that would stand in the way of a just decision are actions that ought not to be performed to begin with: "When advocacy is thus viewed, it becomes clear by what principle limits must be set to partisanship. The advocate plays his role well when zeal for his client's cause promotes a wise and informed decision of the case. He plays his role badly and trespasses on the obligations of professional responsibility, when his desire to win leads him to muddy the headwaters of decision, when, instead of lending a needed perspective to the controversy, he distorts and obscures its true nature."[38]

CONCEPTIONS OF AN ADVERSARY SYSTEM:
THE BROADER CONTEXT

A final category of considerations we can attend to in identifying the elements one may draw on for constructing a view of an adversary system of justice is that of the broader, social context of which it is a part. Fuller, as we already noted, sees adjudication as a form of social ordering, and as it turns out on his analysis, adjudication of the adversary sort is the norm with deviations from it pointing to deficient systems. On his view, partisan advocacy becomes a *sine qua non* in the structuring of a society; it is, he tells us, "an indispensable part of a larger ordering of affairs. The institution of advocacy is not a concession to the frailties of human nature, but an expression of human insight in the design of a social framework within which man's capacity for impartial judgment can attain its fullest realization."[39] While this way of seeing the adversary system offers a justification for it, a point we shall turn to soon, we can here make a few more observations about Fuller's insights into the nature of such a system. Fuller brings out that, in general, there are two main ways of organizing a society, either one of which is needed for the existence of a society: "organization by common aims" and "organization by reciprocity."[40] An example Fuller gives of the first involves people pooling their resources to deal with shared problems and, of the second, people trading crops so that all are better off.[41] Now, adjudication, which Fuller identifies as *a* form of social ordering, has characteristics that the basic forms do not themselves display, namely, "the presentation of proofs and reasoned arguments."[42] "Adjudication is, then," Fuller tells us, "a device which gives formal and institutional expression to the influence of reasoned argument in human affairs. As such it assumes a burden of rationality not borne by any other form of social ordering."[43]

Lieberman sees the adversary approach to settling disputes as a reflection of the adversary mentality of the people of the American frontier and as quite compatible with the conditions of the time: "The adversary legal system...mirrored and supplemented the underlying adversariness of a people not bound to timeless traditions."[44] He brings out how the ethic of the lawyer's having a paramount duty to the client "was admirably suited to the political, economic, and social conditions of frontier America. In early laissez-faire days, comparatively few interactions among people led to disputes serious enough to require courts to resolve them. When disputes that could not be compromised did arise, moreover, they almost always pitted one man against another; strangers to the immediate transaction were rarely affected by the quarrel or its settlement."[45]

Belliotti, too, asks us to understand the appropriateness of the adversary approach relative to a particular form of social ordering, in his case, the libertarian ideology in which "the primacy of the individual is upheld by the zealous advocacy of attorneys representing one and only one of the participants."[46] But unlike Lieberman, who directly attributes adversariness to the nature of the people of the American frontier, Belliotti claims that "the adversary system reflects a certain view of social life: isolated, essentially rational, autonomous individuals interacting only minimally and by free choice. The state is seen as an alien, dangerous force of which intrusions must be limited and powers limited."[47]

Kutak strikes the distinction between a collective and a competitive society to demonstrate how an adversary system of justice, although not necessarily a part of a competitive society, fits well with other of its institutions. "The fact that our society has so many competitive institutions does not, of course, mean that we *must* have an adversary system of justice. But it does suggest that the adversary system of justice reflects the same deep seated values we place on competition among economic suppliers, political parties, and moral and political ideas. It is an individualistic society."[48] In the collective society the path to the common good is paved by the cooperative efforts of the citizens, whereas in the competitive society it is achieved by individual efforts where each assumes no legal responsibility for the competence of others as all interact. Thus, just with regard to rules for disclosure of information during legal proceedings in these societies, we would expect full disclosure in collectivist society and quite otherwise in the competitive. "As a general rule," says Kutak, "there is no duty to disclose facts to other individuals or to the state,"[49] although this is within a context where honesty, truthful answers, and correct information that is volunteered are assumed.[50]

Donagan has us conceive of the adversary system as being, in effect, a system within a system within a system. "The adversary system is a sub-system within many juridical systems themselves being sub-systems within social systems."[51] He illustrates the nature of some conceivable socio-juridical systems telling us that they may be unjust because the laws are such that the trying of some cases always favors a certain side or because the rich can prevail by financially exhausting the poor. These illustrations suggest that a socio-juridical system is one where the structure of society bears directly on the outcome of the litigation. While we are given no examples or definition of a social system of which the adversary system is a part, we might infer from what we have been told about socio-juridical systems that the social system structures social relations within the society that, in turn, have more direct bearing on the adversary system. Thus, we may have a social system where advancement is by merit only, which in itself says little about how justice will be meted out. Such a system, however, may underlie the creation of some state of affairs where there are rich and poor classes, where the rich generally exploit the poor, and ultimately where the rich may prevail, whether at a trial or in any other form of competition within the society, by financially exhausting the poor.

To sum up, we have surveyed what various theorists have

identified as the elements of an adversary approach to justice. We have seen how, with regard to its basic setting, the analyses focused on party participation, including its interested and active nature, the passivity of the arbiter, the use of rational argumentation, the presence of rules structuring the setting, the forensic nature of the setting, and the extent to which truth is a product of the system. Regarding the adversary approach's operation, we considered the dimensions of competent and zealous representation along with the competition of parties. And a consideration of the adversary approach in its broader context acquainted us with the idea of its being a form of social ordering, as indicative of a frontier mentality or of a libertarian ideology, its being compatible with a competitive society, and its being part of a socio-juridical and social system.

As has been urged, the varying descriptions of an adversary approach must first be made evident to cut against the prevailing view that we are dealing with some given phenomenon easily known and easily described. Indeed, each of the theorists considered presents his or her understanding of the adversary system with little or no consideration given to possible alternatives. Once the full scope of the variables is known, readers interested in doing so can reflectively select those that seem most reasonably to depict an adversary environment. As the reader has been presented with a view of human nature that paves the way for constructing a view of self and of roles, so too does the invitation stand for a view of environments, here of the adversary system. A consideration of the justifications for and criticisms of adversary approaches can now be undertaken to assist the reader with this project. At the close of this discussion, an example is given of how one may draw on all of this information and how it becomes relevant for determining lawyers' obligations in an adversary system.

JUSTIFICATIONS FOR ADVERSARY APPROACHES

Let us begin with the justifications for adversary approaches and classify them as consequentialist, where the justification primarily hinges on the good consequences that flow from the approach; non-consequentialist, where something other than the consequences is appealed to in justifying the approach; and comparative, where the justification invokes a comparison of approaches. As for the consequentialist justifications, one group focuses on the good consequences the system produces as regards the immediate outcome of a particular case. The fact that truth or justice will be reached is the crux of the justification.

In this regard we find such statements as "the adversary system is best seen as an attempt to combine truth discovery and procedural fairness,"[52] "presentation of opposing sides in the strongest terms possible before an impartial body is seen as an effective way of arriving at truth and justice,"[53] and "out of that battle, adversary rationale maintains, the truth will be revealed. This is sometimes called the fighting theory of justice, and it underlies both the conceptual framework and the procedure of our law."[54] Part of the reason for thinking that truth and justice will result is that a separation of functions cuts against the possibility of there being bias on the part of the judges from some single-minded line of inquiry that the inquisitorial system invites.[55]

Another group of consequentialist justifications has us attend to the good that comes from the various mechanisms of the approach that provides the foundation for the desired outcome; the quality of the evidence presented and its ultimate utility in ascertaining the facts are pointed to as the good that flows from adversary mechanisms. The idea here is that we can expect advocates in an adversary system, especially those at a disadvantage, to work more diligently for their causes than those in an inquisitorial system; and, if so, we can expect that the quality of the evidence, all in all, will be better.[56]

Third, some consequentialist justifications point to such desirable consequences of adversary adjudication for social organization as the curtailing of the state's power over the individual and social acceptance of the decision. As for the former benefit, it has been brought out that Anglo-American legal history shows the adversary approach to be a "rampart against government tyranny"[57] and that "the goal of zealous advocacy in criminal defense is to curtail the power of the state over its citizens."[58] Social acceptance of the decision seems primarily to be a function of party participation in that the parties' role in choosing a forum, constructing the case, and conducting the process leads to outcomes that fit the needs of the litigants. "Party control...promotes litigant and societal acceptance of decisions rendered by courts,"[59] says Landsman.

The nonconsequentialist justifications appeal to how the adversary approach contributes to preserving the rights and dignity of the individual and to how it is required by the Constitution. The feature of adversary adjudication's being tailored to the parties' interests is one ground for thinking that individual rights are reinforced.[60] One commentator identifies as the "standard justification" of the adversary system the proposition that "only in the adversary system is the dignity of every party to a legal proceeding respected."[61] On another's view, it is the feature of zealous advocacy that allows for the emphasis on the individual—"the primacy of the individual is upheld by the zealous advocacy of attorneys representing one and only one of the participants."[62]

And, if one balks at a justification based on the adversary system's revealing truth, one may find more appealing support for the system that focuses on the individual: "The real value of the adversary system...may not be its contribution to truth but its contribution to the ideal of individual autonomy. This is the rationale underlying many rules that obscure the truth, such as the privilege against self-incrimination...."[63]

Lucas draws our attention to what he identifies as an ancient rule of wisdom and justice, *audi alteram partem*, or "listen to the other side." This he cites as the foundation for the adversary system and offers as justifications for the rule itself various of the consequentialist and nonconsequentialist justifications that we have been considering. Apropos of our discussion here, it is brought out how the adversary system insures that we treat the accused not as a thing but as a person: "The need to hear the accused can be seen in another light. If we dispense with it we either are guilty of a logical error, or if not, must be working on the assumption that the accused is not an agent. Only if we are dealing not with a person but with a mere thing, are we logically entitled to count behavior as altogether conclusive."[64]

As to constitutional requirements that seem to make necessary an adversary system of justice, some see the Constitution's language as not specifically requiring an adversary system but as including many of the features of one. For example, Article III's mention of a trial by jury indicates the element of a neutral and passive fact finder that characterizes adversary ways. Too, we find in the Sixth Amendment's granting the accused the right to be confronted with witnesses against them elements of party participation indicative of an adversary set-up as we do in the compulsory process clause that grants defendants the right to present a defense.[65] Others have no difficulty in seeing the language as flat out requiring the adversary system.[66] One writer points to how recent rulings of the Supreme Court virtually equate due process with an adversary trial.[67]

Finally, the comparative grounds that have been offered to support adversary adjudication include Fuller's claim that experienced judges prefer that approach over others[68] and the claim that, as against the inquisitorial system with its inherent problems, the adversary approach is better. The sort of problems associated with the inquisitorial system that an adversary approach is thought to overcome are the minimal roles played by parties and juries, the likelihood of judges acting on their own biases, and the subordination of individual rights to the pursuit of truth.[69]

CRITICISMS OF ADVERSARY APPROACHES

If we find that a discussion of ways of justifying an adversary system assists us in understanding and selecting from the alternatives for constructing a conception of an adversary system, we can turn for similar assistance to a discussion of criticisms of an adversary system. Major criticisms of the adversary system fall into three categories: (1) criticisms suggesting that the emphasis of the adversary system is wrong, given what it is trying to accomplish; (2) criticisms bringing out that injustices arise from the adversary system, some of which result from wrong emphasis mentioned in (1); and (3) criticisms focusing on how the adversary system is outmoded or anachronistic.

As for the first category, it has been brought out that the adversary system promotes a win-lose mentality that is out of place in the pursuit of justice and truth. Such a mentality may be appropriate in the sports arena, but there is a significant disanalogy between that sphere and a system of justice, namely, that great harm may befall some individual in the event of "losing," whereas such is not the case in sports. With a system of justice, we should seek outcomes based on legal merit.[70] This position is echoed in the complaint of Judge Marvin Frankel that, under current circumstances, advocates see winning as their business. He thinks that, at best, the arrival at the truth at a trial is a happenstance and challenges the traditional view that a trial is primarily designed to arrive at the truth.[71] Without complaining specifically about the win-lose nature of the system, another commentator still argues that the adversary system is not designed properly for securing truth and justice and locates the difficulty in zealous advocacy and the tactics therein.[72] Finally, in this category of criticism, belong suggestions that the orientation of listening to the other side brings with it a number of undesirable results, including needless delays, formality, and conflict.[73]

The second category of criticism focuses on the injustices adversary approaches may produce. Among the injustices seen as flowing from the workings of an adversary system of justice, even if each side is equally balanced, are the harm, such as loss of life, property, and freedom, that can befall one because of the overemphasis placed on winning,[74] the extent to which the delays brought on by zealous advocacy mentioned above may be excessive,[75] and the harm likely to result from employing intricate procedures for the attainment of truth and justice.[76] Other injustices include the damage that can result when lawyers see bluffing as not just permissible but necessary in the execution of their duties to further their clients' interests[77] and the specific harms that may result from advocates failing to maintain confidentiality and from a wrong decision being reached.[78]

As for the criticisms of adversary procedures that focus on their failure to be timely, Derek Bok, Harvard University president, charges that, although there is now a trend toward reconciliation and compromise in various arenas of dispute settling, the legal profession persists in orienting its members to conflict.[79] Others bring out that the adversary mentality fosters a black-and-white, childlike ordering of reality in the win-lose mentality it embraces, and so far as this occurs, we find a gross dissimulation of reality.[80] Frontier America is properly the place for an adversary system with its emphasis on the advocate's primary duty being to the client, asserts one commentator, while another suggests its best context is an early American, agrarian society.[81]

ILLUSTRATION OF HOW AN ATTORNEY'S CONCEPTION OF AN ADVERSARY SYSTEM BEARS ON THE ATTORNEY'S OBLIGATIONS

At the close of chapter 2 we illustrated how, when a position is taken as regards the knowledge component in constructing a view of a profession, the constructor incurs certain obligations. Let us engage in a similar undertaking here as regards a construction of an adversary system and focus on the variable of truth's emerging and the rules that attend the constructed conception. As we do so, we will see how various descriptions, criticisms, and justifications of an adversary system come into play.

Suppose you as an attorney are representing a client at a bail hearing. The prosecutor is arguing for a higher bond being set than is customary for the offense, drawing heavily on the fact that the defendant has few ties to the community, a circumstance which decreases the likelihood of the defendant's reporting for his court date. The prosecutor, in building the case, makes no reference to the criminal record of your client which, according to what your client told you, you know to be rather lengthy. You and the prosecutor both know that your client's criminal record is a factor in the judge's decision, but neither of you has had an opportunity to check the official state records. The judge inquires of you if your client has a criminal record. Does being honest with the judge require you to repeat what your client told you about the record? Should you have checked the official record to discover the truth? Should you do anything now to keep the judge ignorant and urge a decision on the information available? In what follows, I bring out how, as the conception of an adversary system is constructed differently, different rules advise us on how to answer these questions. More specifically, we see how rules variously related to truth, rules requiring one to be honest, to discover the truth, to allow the truth to be discovered, and to reveal the truth, become operative in different conceptions of an adversary system.

We saw how some see as an essential feature of an adversary system that truth emerges as the result of combat between the lawyers of opposing sides; the judge, in this metaphor, is the referee. Now, if one accepts that the truth emerges through combat, it would seem that there would be no justification in this adversary set-up for obligating attorneys to reveal any information about their clients' situations that their opponents did not discover; again, such would be superfluous if indeed the truth emerges through the combat. Continuing to explore this sort of an adversary system, we must inquire whether the other rules mentioned above obtain in some form. Now, if the truth is supposed to emerge from the battle, on this conception of the adversary system, it seems clear that the attorney would have an obligation to the court to allow the truth to be discovered by the court as well as to be honest with the court. Moreover, if the truth is a product of the combat, it would seem that, by hypothesis, the single attorney could not be expected to discover the truth about the matter on his or her own. Such, it seems, is the nature of an adversary system predicated on the hypothesis that the truth emerges through the combat.

If one declines to assume that the truth will emerge from the combat, the question arises as to whether the truth of the matters at issue is important to determine. For it seems that one may draw on those accounts that portray the adversary system as a civilized manner of settling disputes in a nonviolent, verbal fashion and as simply a better alternative to allowing members of society physically to fight the matter out. So conceived, with verbal fighting as the counterpart of, and substitute for, physical combat, verbal treachery and distortions of the truth seem to be permissible in, and even part of, such a system. In this conception of the adversary system, it seems clear that none of the rules set out above would apply. Rules requiring honesty, discovery of the truth, allowing the truth to be discovered, and revealing the truth have no relevance here.

A third alternative would be to recognize the value of arriving at the truth of the matter but deny that such will occur simply as the result of the combat. What rules apply in this sort of system? If we deny that the combat is necessary for the truth to emerge, and if we accept that the judges in an adversary system are largely restricted in what they know about the matters at issue to what counsels present, it seems reasonable to see present a rule requiring each attorney to discover the truth of the matters surrounding their clients' situations. Now it seems that, if a value is placed on the truth being discovered, the attorney would have a duty to allow the truth to be learned or discovered by the court, and from that it follows that attorneys are obligated to be honest with the court with regard to what they know about the matters at issue.

We are now left with the question of whether a rule requiring attorneys to reveal all of what they know about their clients' situations to the court or to the opposing party applies in an adversary set-up where one values truth but where one rejects that it will necessarily emerge from the combat. Arguably, if there were such a rule, we would be moving into an inquisitorial system of justice and be straying from the adversary spirit. On this line of reasoning, it seems that to preserve the integrity of an adversary approach where truth is of value, we cannot posit such a duty. Nonetheless, we might reasonably expect that if each side has performed its duty to discover the truth, the court at least has an opportunity to learn about the total situation. And this seems to be quite different from the conception of an adversary system where the assumption is that the truth will emerge through the combat and where, consequently, no positive obligation was placed on either attorney to discover the truth of the matters at issue.

HOW ATTORNEYS' CONCEPTIONS OF THEIR SOCIETIES BEAR ON THEIR SOCIAL OBLIGATIONS

Having illustrated how an understanding of a dominant feature of an attorney's environment—its adversariness and the attorney's conception of this—is relevant to determining some of the attorney's obligations, let us now consider in more detail how broader aspects of this environment, namely, the society within which the attorney practices, bear on the attorney's obligations. As brought out earlier, the basic idea that I argue for is that the conception of society which the attorney constructs is the attorney's reference point for determining his or her social responsibilities. Standard conceptions of societies are no less woolly or open to debate than any one conception of a profession or of an adversary system that we studied, so it is important for attorneys likewise to construct an adequate conception of society to ascertain clearly what rules guide them in this broader context or what their social obligations are.

Consider various candidates for a lawyer's obligations:

1. to promote justice
2. to engage in *pro bono* activities
3. to educate the lay about the legal system
4. to improve the legal system
5. to improve the penal system
6. to make legal services available
7. to uphold the rule of law
8. to protect the rights of the state or its citizens

MAGRITTE, Rene. *Mental Arithmetic.* 1931. © 1992 C. HERSCOVICI/ARS, N.Y.

9. to resolve controversy or conflict
10. to further the goals of the state
11. to further the goals of the society
12. to provide leadership when possible
13. to simplify the law
14. to amass large sums of money that it might "trickle down" to the needy in society.

It is not difficult to isolate debates over specific social obligations of the attorney. For example, much discussed recently is the extent to which lawyers should make legal services available to society. Some argue that, so long as the profession assumes responsibility for this, one need not place the obligation on each member of the bar to provide pro bono services in some form. Others, taking issue with this argument, say that the true spirit of law as a profession cannot emerge if certain members of the bar can be exempt from any orientation of service. Both sides of the debate, however, seem to be in agreement that services should be made available, even to the poor, with the point of contention being how to effect this. As an initial insight into the thesis I argue for, I can suggest, with this example, that the point of agreement therein is indicative of no hard and fast truth about the profession's obligations *simpliciter* but rather involves how attorneys conceive of their society. Would it not seem incongruous to envision an attorney recognizing such a commitment in a merit society where the principle of distribution of goods, including legal services, was a function not of individual needs but strictly of individual accomplishment and contribution to the society? Again, this example suggests that a conception of the society and not just one of the profession of law guides the attorney's thinking about particular social responsibilities.

Further elucidation of the thesis that attorneys' constructed conceptions of society guide their determination of their social obligations requires a fresh look at our standard conceptions of states, societies, and political organizations together with a recognition that these conceptions are indeterminate and open for construction. Consider some traditional orientations—fascist, contractarian, Marxist, organic, anarchistic. Consider the liberal state, the oligarchic, the democratic, the monarchic, the socialistic. Consider Rawl's conception of the "end state" contrasted with Nozick's historical conception. Consider a state with an adversarial system versus one with an inquisitorial system of justice, a code state versus a common-law state; one where the goods are allocated according to merit, one according to needs, one in an equal fashion, one where individual freedoms are great, one where they are few.

First, I find it less than clear what the intent of the advocates of some of these theories is as regards the inclusiveness of the theory. Consider, for example, the advocate of a society or state with an inquisitorial system of justice. One might, on the one hand, argue that such a system merely represents the fashion in which disputes between citizens or between citizens and the state will be settled and that no commitment to aspects of how the society will further be ordered is thereby made. One the other hand, one might recognize that certain freedoms the citizen would be afforded in a liberal society, like that of an accused's right to remain silent, would not fit easily within an inquisitorial system of justice and that it is thus difficult to adopt such a system without also committing oneself to other aspects of structuring the society. Further, these observations can be made regardless of the question of the intent of the theorist.

Next, it is not always clear whether features usually associated with various theories of state are to be construed as necessary or accidental properties of the state so conceived. For example, a socialist state is commonly conceived as one where communal ownership of land, production capabilities, etc., is the rule, with distribution of goods based on need or a principle of equality. Nonetheless, it is not clear why, in principle, some standard of merit could not be operative for the distribution of all or some goods, recognizing the essence of a socialism to be common ownership without any necessary commitment to the principle of equal or need-based distribution of goods and recognizing further that it is a matter of empirical fact that most socialist states have opted for something other than a merit principle.

These two observations of unclarity are not unrelated. Both are indicative of the conceptual confusion that hovers over various theories of state and just what we are committed to, conceptually, when we identify some state as socialist, fascist, monarchical, and so on. We can recognize that the juxtaposition of elements or features of a society is not so rigidly defined as we may have thought, allowing for conceptions of societies that are more creatively constructed and that are open to emendation. These observations have obvious relevance not merely for the attorney but for anyone, given the common environment of society. They make all of us mindful not only of the broad scope of our constructive endeavors in that they extend to society itself but also of the fashion in which these endeavors bring with them rules to guide our conduct. Attorneys who build a notion of society that includes the feature of its being a huge forum for exchanges of information among citizens for the development of an increasingly enlightened citizenry quite simply put themselves in the world in a different fashion from those attorneys who exclude such a feature. For this feature brings with it normative advice of a general nature for one knowledgeable about the law to educate the lay about the legal system. Similarly, citizens who made this feature a part of their notion of society would be in the world in a fashion different from other citizens; they would consider themselves obligated to communicate with others about matters of which they are knowledgeable.

This completes our look at the ways in which aspects of an attorney's environment, the society in general and an adversary system, contribute to determining an attorney's obligations. We have seen how matters are made complex for attorneys in that neither conceptions of societies nor of aspects of them, like an adversary system of justice, come readily packaged or exist in some invariable form[82] any more than do conceptions of humans or of their roles as professionals and attorneys.

Our study of the attorney's environments gives us a good idea of the range of variables that can enter one's thinking about an environment. Our study of the attorney's environments also demonstrates how the conceptions we construct of environments commit us to ways of acting. If we conceive of a university as a locus for transmitting our cultural heritage, and if we think of our society as being culturally diverse, we examine whether our curriculum includes multicultural perspectives and introduce these perspectives to the curriculum if they are absent. If we think of nature as an active, living, and vulnerable entity, we recycle, conserve and replenish resources, protect endangered species, and identify and strive to eliminate sources of pollution.

Sometimes it seems that the most we can say about the conceptions which we construct of our environments is that the conceptions represent how we choose to see ourselves in various environments. Thus, I may construct a conception of a global community of which all humans are members. I see dialogue as a significant, cohesive force in this community, and I set out to learn a new language as I situate myself in this environment which I have constructed. Here, we may say that I have created an environment for myself or that I have chosen to see myself in the world in a certain fashion. But there is no literal sense in which I have created an environment which others can or must occupy.

At other times as we guide ourselves with a conception of an environment, we literally create an environment for others. As a professor, I may conceive of the classroom as a place for learning to occur through ongoing exchanges between the professor and students; I thus refrain from lecturing and encourage students to discuss the reading assignment. My conception of the classroom environment creates an environment for all of us present; no one in my classroom listens to a lecture for the entire hour.

But even where our construction of an environment seems to entail nothing more than how we choose to see ourselves in our environment, our conception has the potential for creating an environment for others. As others imitate me as I act in my global community, a global community emerges. So our constructions and our actions, coupled with the hypothesis of role modeling, have significance not just for me and my world but for others and their worlds. Mindful of the phenomenon of role modeling, I am cautious to construct roles and environments that have me act only in ways which I am willing for others to imitate. Role modeling evidently becomes important for us as role constructors when we realize that our constructed conceptions guide us in a social context. What remains for us to consider is how these considerations about role modeling allow us to delineate our universal ethic more fully and why the hypothesis of role modeling is viable.

Brothers, run your joyous race, hero-like to conquest flying.

van BEETHOVEN, Ludwig. *Symphony No. 9 in D Minor* (Choral), *Op. 125.* Deutsche Staatsbibliothek, Berlin in der Stiftung Preussischer Kulturbesitz, Musikabteilung.

5

▼

The Contours of the Universal Ethic
Its Nature, Scope, and Limits

This concluding chapter explores how role models are significant for specifying further the nature of our general ethical theory. I draw on role modeling to identify important restrictions on our constructive endeavors together with the scope of these endeavors. I then turn to general experience, philosophy, and psychology to develop support for the hypothesis of role modeling and in doing so deepen our thinking about modeling.[1] What seems quite inconclusive about the phenomenon of role modeling when looked at in a piecemeal fashion emerges as a viable network of ideas on modeling that proves useful for establishing an important component of our universal ethic.

RELEVANCE OF MODELING
FOR OUR THEORY OF
HUMAN NATURE AND ETHICS

This simple notion, that I obtain from others, by observing their activity, ideas about the sort of person I wish to be or about qualities to imitate, and that they similarly obtain such things from me, is closely related to our theory of human nature. We saw how people are to develop, in an ongoing, reflective process, conceptions of themselves as humans and as persons in varying roles and environments.

141

When we attend to the ways we influence each other's behavior, we are able both to identify an important source for our conceptions of ourselves and to place some important restrictions on the sort of persons we might choose to become. Our actions occur in a social context and have social significance. So we allow ourselves to become the sort of persons we are and act as we do only to the extent we are willing for others to use us as models; the extent to which we deviate from this restriction is one ground on which other people may fairly criticize us for being that sort of person or for acting in that fashion. Further, as other people can cite reasons why we are serving as bad role models, they can fairly criticize us on another ground, for the social reality is a shared reality, and all people have a legitimate concern for how each person's conduct affects the behavior of other people. As we develop our conceptions of our roles and environments, we implicitly endorse these as good conceptions, for they are the products of choices we made about how best to build these conceptions. Our warranty of their value for general social use reflects their meeting the test of our best judgment, which is important, but not determinative for their evaluation given that they may be used by other people.

Now, our criterion for evaluating conduct is a criterion similar to the Golden Rule and to the Kantian standard in that the touchstone of correctness of action is the individual's willingness to allow others to act similarly. But our abilty here to cast our criterion in terms of role modeling and imitative behavior and to locate it in a social context enables us to avoid, in large measure, some of the difficulties typically associated with those other experiments with consistency criteria; for example, a common criticism is that it seems fanatics can justify their outrageous activity and evade criticism from others if they are willing, in a consistent fashion, to allow others to act likewise. These other criteria seem insufficiently to create a social context within which we can begin to explore the difficulties with the fanatic's activity. For these other criteria seem to create an unreal or artificial circumstance of the agent's willingness to be in a world where all others are acting likewise, or where such activity is being directed at the agent by others, regardless of any possibility or likelihood of this occurring. Our criterion immediately locates the agent in a social context where the dynamics of role modeling and imitative behavior establish the real possibility of this activity influencing the conduct of others. While this introduction of a social context is no absolute check on what activity one might will to become universal, it does ensure that the agent think in more concrete and realistic ways about the contemplated conduct. Also, as we brought out above, even if people are willing for others to use them as models, they are not immune from further evaluation by others in their social reality.

The same advice that limits our constructions of our nature, roles, and environments indicates the scope of these constructions. Looked at negatively, the advice restricts us from adopting constructions which we believe make us bad role models. Looked at positively, the advice, by requiring us to think of ourselves as role models for others, in effect requires us to be concerned with improving our social reality. Our constructed conceptions, as products of our fully reflective attitudes, represent our judgments on how best to conceive of our nature, roles, and environments. As we endorse others inimating us as we use these conceptions to guide us, we envision a better world. Once we start thinking about responsible human agency in this fashion—where individuals show a concern for how their conduct will be influencing the conduct of others and take that influence as a relevant factor in deciding how to act themselves—it seems we are already very much in the domain of moral education, for a primary motivation for developing any such theory would be this concern for the moral development of others, and we would expect any such theory to provide an account of how this can be done—how the educator's actions can help to bring about the desired actions of the person being educated.

In effect our universal ethic implicitly endorses a position on moral education in its use of the phenomenon of role modeling. Our concern with others imitating us and our acceptance of the reality of modeling addresses the issues of what we are trying to convey to others as well as how we will convey it. So role modeling obviously figures prominently in our universal ethic both with regard to how we should act and to how we can and do influence the conduct of others. At issue now is the viability of the hypothesis of role modeling. I turn to general experience, philosophy, and psychology and draw on the pervasiveness of role modeling in these areas to establish its significance and strength.

SUPPORT FOR ROLE MODELING

Role Modeling in General Experience

Upon analysis, we can see that the significance that our universal ethic attaches to role modeling is not without parallel in general experience and in other theories of ethics and moral development. The phenomenon of role modeling evidently is as pervasive in experience as it is in theorizing about experience.

Drawing, to begin with, on what our own experiences suggest, it seems that some people become the sort of individuals that they are, many of them shallow, without form, growing little and having limited opportunities for growth, because theirs is a world populated by similar people. The self-perpetuating nature of this syndrome seems to result from there being too few people in their environments worth imitating. For models they turn to what television and movies have to offer. Sometimes these media portray people caught up in situations of a hopelessly whimsical nature, in which case the model for living becomes the person who parades through life in a carefree fashion, always ready to deliver the most appropriate one-line quip that generates spontaneous, uproarious laughter; in a survey conducted in 1987, high school students identified the actor and comedian Eddie Murphy as their top hero. Sometimes portrayed are people with the most pressing of human problems that somehow become defined and resolved in a very short order, in which case the model has us aspire to leading lives where the problems are of just that tractable nature, where resolutions have at last caught up with the speed and efficiency of fast food, word processing, and jet travel. Such portrayals may serve as models and guide our conduct to some limited extent but can never serve us well given the narrow range of human activities to which they apply.

Others seem to live in or seek out an enriched environment and are influenced by wise and creative people who are ever growing, and who are fresh from learning new things, from acquiring new abilities and developing the old, and whose characters are deepened by experience. On this line of reasoning, it is no accident that, in the realm of occupational roles, the best of our scholars, students, lawyers, and artists associate with or have had the opportunity to mingle with those who excel in living their lives creatively. Hume spoke of daily imitation of the great writers as his method for the development of his own writing skills. Plato, concerned that citizens place reason in control of their desires and will, sought to keep artists out of the well-formed society. He said that artists portrayed deviant personalities, people whose reasoning had been overpowered by their desires or will, and argued that the citizens would become more like these sorts if exposed to them in the theater. Put differently, he wanted only good models for the citizens.

Consider also the way in which some customs and some religions influence conduct at a distance by planting in people's minds examples of good behavior through their portrayals of saints and folk heroes or their counterparts. Benjamin Franklin advises us to imitate Socrates and Jesus. In his novel *Fifth Business*,[2] Robertson Davies casts his main character as one who, convinced that he has seen the workings of a saint, seeks to convince others of this person's sainthood and to learn all he can about saints. The subject affords Davies a number of opportunities to comment on saints and on people's relationships. One woman in the novel, for example, takes great pleasure in thinking about Saint Francis, whose gentleness induced wild birds to perch on him. She sees him as a model for ordinary people and as an ideal against which she can evaluate others. In a sense, people's selecting personal saints may serve the psychological function of keeping before them figures whose positive qualities they are willing to endorse and would want others likewise to endorse.

Further, if we look more broadly to our beliefs and experiences about learning, the hypothesis of modeled activity explains much, or looked at from a different perspective, is confirmed by our common experiences, which confirmation is another ground for adopting a hypothesis. Consider how, generally, in cases where we are learning to follow rules or acquire some skill or habit, models often play a part. I doubt very much that I would end up speaking like a fluent speaker of some language were I merely given all of the rules governing the language and expected to learn the language without ever hearing it spoken or having the benefit of imitating a native speaker. And the same seems to hold true for learning to play a complex game or a musical instrument. Some model of competence seems important for guiding my development in these areas. And turning from situations where we are trying to acquire some behavior to situations where we simply do learn certain behaviors as a matter of course, the thesis of modeling seems no less useful in explaining what we encounter, nor is it any the less confirmed by these experiences of passive or unconscious learning, whether they entail imitation of figures in advertising, friends and colleagues, a folk hero or saint, or a character or performer.

Role Modeling in Philosophy

Let us now turn to philosophy's legacy of views on ethics and moral education for further support for the hypothesis of role modeling. We find that the various theories that we consider seem either tacitly to assume such a hypothesis or become stronger by adopting it as an auxiliary hypothesis.

Plato first raised many of the questions in ethics and moral education that still concern us: What is virtue? Can it be taught? If so, how do we teach it? As we will see, Aristotle was in fundamental disagreement with his mentor, Plato, at least with regard to how these questions should be answered. This ancient controversy between Plato and Aristotle lives in the contemporary discussions of whether one's moral development is primarily a question of one's acquiring knowledge and learning to think correctly about moral matters or of acquiring the proper habits. Put slightly differently, one may see the main question as whether the teaching of morals is more like teaching mathematics and history or more like teaching one to play a musical instrument. Plato has come to stand for emphasizing the cognitive element in moral development, and Aristotle, the habitual.

In his dialogue *Meno*, Plato identifies and explores some of the questions mentioned above. Early in the dialogue Socrates indicates that some order can be found in the apparent multiplicity of virtues or moral qualities like honesty, obedience, trustworthiness; they can be distilled to the virtues of temperance and justice. In his conversation with Meno, Socrates speaks of the "sameness" of all virtues to temperance and justice.[3] As the dialogue progresses, we find further that, although virtue is a type of knowledge or wisdom, it cannot be taught. Socrates at one point refers to it as a gift of the gods.[4] But even if the wisdom that allows us to be good is a gift of the gods and cannot be taught, that does not mean that whether people are good or bad is beyond human control. For earlier in the dialogue Socrates introduces his view that the human soul is immortal and that each soul contains the wisdom of the ages; each soul has seen all things and knows of all things including virtue. Learning, then, does not result from teaching but from recollecting.[5]

To support this doctrine of there being knowledge in the mind at birth or of innate knowledge, Plato portrays how Socrates is able to draw some principles of geometry from the mind of a slave who previously had no formal instruction in geometry; supposedly this knowledge was in the slave's mind all along, and he merely needed someone like Socrates to jog his memory in order "to bring it to a conscious level."[6] Socrates points out that part of this process of inquiring, learning, and recollecting involves one's recognizing one's ignorance, becoming perplexed, and desiring to know. The upshot of this, we gather, is that virtue, being a type of knowledge, also can be recollected. The role of the moral educator, then, at most is to help the student recollect, much as Socrates assisted the slave, since the moral educator does not teach the student something that the student did not already know. To the extent Socrates embodies the virtues of willingness to admit ignorance and desire to acquire knowledge, it seems that, if the student is to attain the requisite frame of mind in order to recollect, that of recognizing one's ignorance and desiring to know, the student is to become like Socrates in that regard—the moral educator cannot teach but can serve as a role model. Looked at in this way, it seems that Socrates's account assumes the hypothesis of role modeling. Looked at from a different perspective, it seems that the absence in Socrates's account of any clear procedure for instilling the requisite frame of mind in the student suggests the utility of adopting role modeling as an auxilary hypothesis.

A complete alternative to the Platonic position is Aristotle's view that habit formation is central to becoming virtuous or moral. We do not recollect knowledge latent in our minds and thus learn of virtue as Plato thought. Nor are we born virtuous. Rather, we practice doing various types of acts to acquire the corresponding virtue; we become just by acting justly over and over; brave, by acting bravely. Just as we learn to play a musical instrument by actually playing and practicing it and developing a habit, so too with the acquisition of virtue. Attending to the specifics of Aristotle's position, we find him defining virtue as "a state of character concerned with choice, lying in a mean, i.e. the mean relative to us, this being determined by a rational principle...; it is a mean between two vices."[7] On Aristotle's view, most virtues are the proper disposition for us to be in with regard to a spectrum of related dispositions, with the extremes signifying vices. Thus, with regard to fear and confidence, we would say that the one who is in a virtuous state is the courageous person, who is midway between the extremes represented by the person who is rash—the person who has too much confidence—and the person who is cowardly—the person who has too little.[8]

In developing as moral agents, we are to strive to attain the midpoint as it applies or is relevant to our circumstances. Thus, with regard to sharing one's money, the proper disposition to be in is generosity, which is midway between extravagance and stinginess. But being generous for the poor person may entail the donation of moneys in an amount less than the donation by the generous person who is wealthy. So we describe this situation as one where each has found the mean relative to him or her with regard to sharing one's riches. The process by which one acquires the correct disposition or identifies the relative mean is one of performing actions that fall in that category; one gets in the habit of doing these things.[9]

Consider how Aristotle's advice to the developing moral agent about arriving at the mean that constitutes virtue can not only be cast in terms of models but, arguably, is clearer, more plausible, and more in line with other aspects of his philosophizing when cast in these terms. For example, if we are to acquire the virtue of generosity, we are to aim at the mid-point between the extremes of stinginess and extravagance. In terms of modeling, we are to develop a symbol of what a generous person in our situation would be like and imitate that. If we are far off center to begin with—say we are very stingy—then it may require our imitating what seem to be the actions of an extraordinarily extravagant person in order to get our actions to be generous as a matter of fact. Stating Aristotle's advice to cultivate habits of virtue in terms of striving to be like the person who has the qualities I wish to acquire seems to fit well with his position that essences only exist in particular things, that there is no generosity per se but only generous people.

Lawrence Kohlberg, a contemporary psychologist/philosopher, dubs his theory of moral education a Platonic approach. He rejects the Aristotelian method that requires one's acquiring a panoply of virtues though habituation, pointing out, among other things, that such virtues as honesty simply do not exist. Findings of psychologists, Kohlberg tells us, indicate that no one is totally honest, that everyone cheats to a certain degree, and that there is, consequently, no virtue of honesty.[10] The task of moral education, as Kohlberg sees it, is to acquaint the child with a single concept, namely, justice.[11] He thus aligns himself with Plato's characterization of moral education as a task of acquiring knowledge and, further, with Plato's denial that we must learn of a multiplicity of virtues.

Now, Kohlberg identifies six stages of moral development based on his cross-cultural investigations. When people reach the highest stage, they fully understand what the requirements for acting justly are. Even at the lowest stage, Kohlberg indicates, the child has some dim perception of what justice is. The moral educator is to determine the student's current stage of moral development and boost the student to the next stage where the student will grasp more clearly the demands of justice. The process continues until the highest stage is reached. To advance the student to a higher level, the moral educator is to create in the child what Kohlberg refers to as "cognitive conflict." This parallels the perplexity that Socrates sought to generate in Meno's slave in order to stimulate inquiry. In Kohlberg's view, when the child is presented with the shortcomings and limitations of his or her present level of moral development and is pointed in the direction of the next stage, the child will enter a temporary state of perplexity, and having considered the matter, the child will restore mental order and ascend to a higher stage of moral development.[12]

Talk of modeling in the statement of Kohlberg's position also seems to make more explicit his conception of the dynamics of moral education. When the student is presented with a dilemma that seems perplexing because of the state of development that the student is in, we might say that the student develops a sense of a person that the student does not wish to be like; that confrontation with a negative model leads to the development of a concept of a person that the student does wish to imitate, and that conception is of the agent acting in accord with a higher level on the ladder of moral development. Thus, consider a student who is at stage two of moral education, where the right action is conceived of as what furthers one's own interest. Suppose the problem is presented that some other person has some cookies and that person does not wish to share them, but the student would very much like to be offered some. The student is asked whether self-interest should always control. To the extent the student sees the limitations of wanting to be like the person with the cookies and now considers being like the person at the next stage of moral development where the right act is conceived of as what conforms to group expectations, we might fruitfully introduce talk of modeling into Kohlberg's account.

To this point, the Platonic and Aristotelian positions in moral education have been portrayed as mutually exclusive. Indeed, we saw how Kohlberg found it incumbent upon him to argue against Aristotle in arguing for his Platonic view. And our earlier dealings with Plato's and Aristotle's theories characterized them as rival hypotheses. Frankena challenges the assumption of the incompatibility of the approaches and attempts to conjoin them and thereby offer a third major alternative.

He recognizes that moral education, in part, requires the transmission of knowledge and, in part, the creation of habits and other dispositions to incline the individual to do what the individual knows is right. Such a view, Frankena points out, overcomes the knowledge-action objection associated with Platonic theory. Ensuring that people do what they know is right is just as important an aspect of moral education as ensuring that one knows what is right, according to Frankena. And moral education itself is a single, integrated process during which both of these aspects of the process are transmitted at each step of the way.[13]

R. S. Peters also creates an amalgam of the Aristotelian and Platonic theories.[14] He endorses the view that the mature moral agent embraces principles that are rationally justifiable and, further, that this agent intelligently applies this moral code. In this respect his view is Platonic. But he also recognizes that, based upon what we know of the child's mental development, the child is unable to cognize such rationally justifiable principles, let alone intelligently apply them. In this Peters finds a paradox. We want children to become mature moral agents, but children are incapable in their formative years of understanding or living the lives of such agents. It is here that habit plays a role. Children are capable of forming habits that will induce them to act as mature moral agents do, and the development of such habits in children is the aim of the first phase of moral education; in this concern with the moral habits of children consists the Aristotelian component of Peters's view. It is only later in the child's moral development that moral principles and their application are introduced; here we see the introduction of the Platonic aspect of the theory. So, whereas the Aristotelian and Platonic aspects of moral education occur at the same time on Frankena's combination of them, they occur *seriatim* for Peters.

If it makes sense to see as operative in the views of Plato and Aristotle a theory of role models, it makes similar sense to do so with regard to Frankena's and Peters's positions. For we saw how each could be construed as a contemporary attempt to wed the Platonic and Aristotelian views. More specifically, we can cast Frankena's and Peters's talk of developing habits in children in terms of children imitating people with these habits. We can cast their talk of educating children to guide their conduct with rational principles in terms of children seeing people who follow moral rules as role models. Not only is the hypothesis of role modeling compatible with Frankena's and Peters's accounts but its addition to their accounts also strengthens them. These accounts are silent on the mechanism whereby children acquire habits and learn to guide their conduct with rules, and the hypothesis of role modeling can provide that mechanism.

Evident from this brief look at some of the major philosophical contributions to the theory of moral development is the fashion in which the debate has focused basically on whether reason, habit, or both is the essence of moral education. Obscured by this preoccupation with assessing which of these variables, admittedly major, is correct is the importance that role modeling seems to hold for all these views. If it is fair to attribute the thesis of role modeling to major theories of moral education,[15] it seems we can use that fact in establishing the viability of the thesis. Establishing this viability is important, since the thesis of role modeling figures prominently in our universal ethic which requires our willingness for others to use us as a role model when we act in accord with our constructed conceptions.

Role Modeling in Psychology

Among social-learning theorists, Albert Bandura is the best known for work on modeled behavior. Observations he makes in his writings accord with what some of our common-sense speculations suggested above. Says, Bandura, "It is evident from informal observation that human behavior is transmitted, whether deliberately or inadvertently, largely through exposure to social models."[16] He goes on to say that it "is difficult to imagine a culture in which language, mores, vocational activities, familial customs, and educational, religious, and political practices are gradually shaped in each new member by direct consequences of their trial-and-error performances without benefit of models who display these cultural patterns in their behavior."[17]

Let us attend more closely to the contours of the thesis of role modeling from the perspective of psychology, considering first the general parameters of the phenomenon and then the theoretical attempts to account for it. Conditions under which modeling occurs, in Bandura's view, include an observational, a remembering, and an action stage. During the observational stage, it is important that what is to be imitated is perceived correctly. Those features chosen for imitation reflect a tendency among people to be discriminating in the behaviors they wish to acquire and to turn to those displayed by prestigious or engaging persons.[18] The significance that a social-learning theorist like Bandura attaches to symbols enters in stage two, where the behavior, usually learned as a whole, is retained in the memory through a symbol of it.[19] Peculiar to the third stage is the translation of the mental entity—the symbol—into the action.[20] While some activities seem possible to acquire only through modeling—like learning a language—others,[21] arguably, are still best acquired by modeling even if other means—like trial and error—are possible. Bandura brings out how modeled activity can be seen to reduce human costs and hazards, increase efficiency, shorten the learning process, and allow for the avoidance of error.[22]

The thesis of role modeling is offered as a contribution to

social-learning theory, an orientation in psychology that stresses the importance of the cognitive domain in explaining and changing behavior and stresses how those with whom we associate largely delimit the scope of our own activity;[23] symbols figure importantly in this realm[24] and, to the extent people fix in their minds with symbols specific behaviors they wish to imitate, so too do role models. Social-learning theorists consider their orientation to be a major alternative to those moves in psychology that eschew mental entities in accounting for behavior, whether these come from stimulus-response theorists, who use only environmental stimuli and the organism's responses in their work, or from behaviorists, who are not wedded to stimuli and responses as being the sole entities we have to work with but still are committed to external, measurable actions and events as being the grist for the explanation and alteration of behavior.[25]

Although Bandura finds it surprising that the thesis of role modeling seems absent from traditional accounts of human behavior,[26] given its prevalence in human activity, that is not to say that the thesis is without a history or variations. Bandura brings out that "modeling phenomena," as he prefers to call what is usually classified under "imitation" and "identification," have been differentiated and classified in a variety of ways, with some of the descriptors including "learning by example," "observational learning," "identification," "internalization," "copying," "contagion," and "role taking."[27] At the turn of the century, theorists like Morgan, Tarde, and McDougall speculated that the phenomenon of humans imitating one another was instinctual, and Tarde, in his *The Laws of Imitation*,[28] suggested that our behavior generally is a function of imitation, both conscious and subconscious. Subsequent development of the thesis turned on a rejection of the instinctual foundation of modeling and a modification of its scope. Some, for example, stressed that imitation occurs only when one acts in accord with a conscious desire. In 1941, Miller and Dollard, in their *Social Learning and Imitation*,[29] indicated that the behavior selected for imitation is that of a superior person, and that, if this person is imitated, rewards will ensue. Piaget explored how children engage in make-believe, imitative behavior to help themselves adjust to new situations and aspects of the adult world that seem frightening or threatening to them.[30]

Rejecting the theory of human nature that grounds modeling in instinct, Bandura posits a theory of human nature from the perspective of the social learning theorist: "...human nature is characterized as a vast potentiality that can be fashioned by direct and vicarious experiences into a variety of forms within biological limits."[31] Further, we find that within the scope of modeling is not just the reproduction of specific behaviors but the production of those that are innovative. Says Bandura, "By observing a model of the desired behavior, an individual forms an idea of how specific response components must be combined and temporally sequenced to produce new behavioral configurations."[32] Commenting further on the domain of modeling, Bandura points to its possible use for rule-guided behavior[33] and for the development of moral judgments.[34]

It is worth commenting at this point on the similarities between this view of human nature and that which we developed earlier. In portraying people as constructors of rule-referring conceptions of themselves, we are in line with the social-learning theorist's view insofar as both views reject any fixed human essence, and both grant wide latitude for the development of the self. Recognizing this similarity, we can say that, on independent grounds based on empirical evidence, social-learning theory offers a view of human nature similar to one we derived primarily on philosophical grounds. Looked at from a slightly different perspective, our theory gains support from another discipline. The differences between these views of human nature, however, are noteworthy. It is not simply a matter of psychology and philosophy speaking with a single voice, nor is it a matter of the ability of these disciplines to operate independently without informing one another. For one thing, our view essentially ties the conceptions we develop for ourselves to rules for conduct, whereas the connection seems far more tenuous on the hypothesis of the social-learning theorist. Further, our theory of human nature made no direct references to modeling, although, like most of the philosophical contributions to moral education surveyed above, it seems to be strengthened by this hypothesis, which is part and parcel of the social-learning theorist's view of how these innovative personality configurations are created. We can recall that we identified as grist for the construction of self such things as personality types we directly perceive and those we encounter in fiction and in historical, biographical, and autobiographical accounts. Cast in terms of the thesis of modeling, our selection of these materials for self-construction can be described as our wish to imitate these people or some of their qualities.

In summary, I have taken seriously the project of establishing the viability of the hypothesis of role modeling. For this hypothesis is an important component of our ethic which requires us to be willing for others to use us as a role model. I have eschewed facile moves like invoking how obvious role modeling is to urge its acceptance. Such moves obscure the nature of the phenomenon and do nothing to assist the reader for whom the phenomenon is not obvious. As we turned to general experience, philosophy, and psychology for support for the hypothesis, we not only found reasons to endorse the hypothesis but also became better acquainted with the nature of role modeling.

THE CONTOURS OF THE UNIVERSAL ETHIC

Let us take a final look at what the view amounts to. The claim is that we are to take an active role in assessing and contructing who we are. Our doing so ranges from the most general condition, circumstance, or role we find ourselves in, our being human, to the more specific circumstance of being a member of a particular occupation, of having a certain status within a family, of our being a citizen, an adherent of some religion, and so on. Our construction of our roles and of who we are includes our environments at least insofar as it includes how we conceive of ourselves in our environments, so we can speak of our roles broadly as encompassing our environments. Further, there is nothing that precludes us from breaking from the traditional categories that cast us in certain roles which we are to think critically about; our thinking may go more deeply to the question of whether there is some circumstance of our lives that as yet has gone undefined, let alone been critically assessed and constructed by us.

The advice for conduct that we obtain from these principled conceptions can be looked at as comprising interacting constellations since, evidently, we are citizens as we are humans, and we are workers as we are citizens; we belong to families as we work in various settings, and we live in societies as we work in these various settings. I am always mindful of the range of roles I have constructed and continue to assess; I am one person striving to act as a whole person, which inevitably means recognizing that, when conflicts arise in what my roles advise, I must evaluate and decide how best to act. While some roles and their related rules may generally seem more important than others and may generally take precedence over others, these more significant roles need not always prevail.

This is a far more sophisticated model for thinking about ourselves as human agents than any we have heretofore drawn on; it is a model that helps us realize that the juggling of our commitments regarding how we see ourselves and of the clusters of rules that go along with each of the roles we occupy is a very complex matter; our diverging roles and obligations call for ongoing reassessment, for deliberation over conflicts, and for decisions about how to resolve conflict, whether to revise a conception of a role, or to let the dictates of one give way to those of another. In a way, we are like judges when they must decide which of the opposing parties prevails when each party invokes a principle important to the entire legal system.

But our task as human agents is, in some important sense, more difficult than a judge's. Not only is it incumbent on us to resolve conflict, but we must recognize the problem to begin with. We have the responsibility for developing the conceptions and rules that may give rise to difficulties. We must bring the rules and resolutions of their conflicts to bear on our own activity. Further, as we govern our experience, we have the opportunity to see the impact of our decisions on others, to receive criticism or praise from them, and to see the extent to which our constructed roles have contributed to desireable and undesirable modes of conduct among others; and we have opportunities immediately to reassess our decisions and actions for the future.

We are mindful that our views of ourselves and of our environments are both the result of modeling and the subject matter for modeling. As such, we can say that part of the project of morally educating people is to ensure that there are good models to imitate. We bear primary responsibility for educating ourselves both collectively and individually. Each person is a potential model for another, so we ought always to consider whether we are willing for others to imitate our chosen actions. This line of thinking places individuals in the position of being concerned with their own moral education and with that of others, for it acknowledges that we learn from each other as we create our roles and environments.

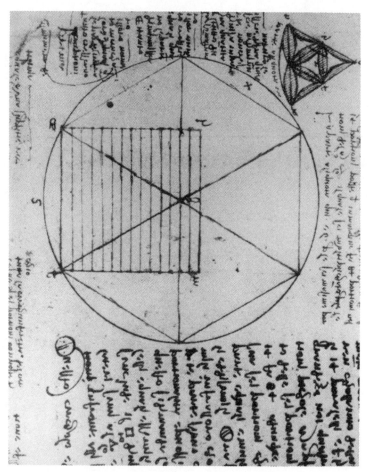

DA VINCI, Leonardo. *Geometric Studies*, *Codex Atlanticus* 111v–a. 1504. Notebook drawing. Biblioteca Ambrosiana, Milan.

Epilogue

Our journey through the forest of silver trees now comes to an end, but where has it taken us? Surely as we deplane, we are a little more familiar with the terrain of legal and general ethics and with how desirable procedural features of legal ethics provide the contours for a universal ethic. We are acquainted with what it means to think of our nature as role constructors. By attending to the professional and lawyer as paradigm cases, we understand now that many variables present themselves for the construction of any of our roles. We saw how we can construct conceptions of the settings in which we find ourselves by analogy with the ways attorneys can construct conceptions of an adversary system and of a society. And we learned how the conceptions we construct bring with them rules that guide our conduct.

The creative undertakings that this book recommends locate it along with some contemporary attempts to break from single, fixed conceptions of human nature. But absent from similar accounts by pragmatists, existentialists, and moral psychologists is any clear connection between these creations or constructions of the self and our moral experience. These accounts are top-heavy on the side of more flexible ways of thinking about our nature and skimpy if not silent on how they bear on conduct. Using the approach to ethics of lawyers as a model, we find rules for conduct tied to the constructions we create. Moreover our universalization criterion stated in terms of role models further serves to integrate our flexible approach to human nature with moral conduct.

If this journey was indeed the intellectual adventure I promised at the outset, it continues. For as role constructors, we are ever assessing and developing conceptions of ourselves and our environments. Much of what before may have seemed to have marginal significance for our personal lives now becomes raw material for our constructive endeavors. We can think of the many books, happenings, people, and ideas that we encounter as presenting a multiplicity of invitations to us for how we think about our roles and our world. More than learning from our experiences, we now make from them.

NOTES

▼

CHAPTER 1

1. Chris Hackler, "Is Medical Ethics Unique?" *Business and Professional Ethics*, vol. 2, nos. 3/4, 1979.

2. Charles Fried, *Right and Wrong* (Cambridge, Mass.: Harvard University Press, 1978), p. 192. Despite the introduction of a variety of general or universal ethical approaches as relevant for legal ethics, David E. Schrader in his *Ethics and the Practice of Law* seems, in the end analysis, to align himself with those thinking there is something essentially different about legal ethics. For one thing, we find that "what constitutes ethical behavior in the legal profession cannot simply be reduced to the goal of promoting justice in society." (Englewood Cliffs, N.J.: Prentice Hall, 1988), p. vii. Schrader has us attend to the attorney's role in the adversary system to understand and justify the lawyer's obligations. (p. 12.) Further, he refers to ethical theory, of which he focuses on Kantianism and utilitarianism, as an "important starting point for legal ethics" (pp. 2, 17–42) and makes no claim that such universal approaches are sufficient for resolving issues of legal ethics. See also Richard Wasserstrom's "Lawyers as Professionals: Some Moral Issues," *Human Rights Quarterly*, vol. 5, no. 1 (1975), pp. 105–128. Here he brings out that an attorney's activities that deviate from ordinary morality are only qualifiedly justified by an attorney's role in the adversary system. For one thing, we must consider whether the institution of which the role is a part is justified.

3. Geoffrey Hazard, *Ethics in the Practice of Law* (New Haven, Conn.: Yale University Press, 1978), p. 3.

4. Felix S. Cohen, "Modern Ethics and the Law," in *The Legal Conscience: Selected Papers of Felix S. Cohen*, edited by Lucy Kramer Cohen (New Haven, Conn.: Yale University Press, 1960).

5. Robert C. Schultz, "On the Meaning and Value of Professionalism," unpublished manuscript, p. 11. Prof. Schultz, now at University of Washington, Bothell Branch, delivered this paper at Calgary University's Summer Institute on Professionalism.

6. B. Freedman, "A Meta-Ethics for Professional Morality," *Ethics*, vol. 89 (October 1978), p. 10.

7. *Professional Responsibility: Problems and Materials*, edited by Thomas D. Morgan and Ronald D. Rotunda (Mineola, N.Y.: The Foundation Press, Inc., 1976), pp. 145–146.

8. Jeremy Bentham, *The Principles of Morals and Legislation* (New York: Hafner Publishing Co., 1948), p. 25.

9. Hazard, p. 5.

10. John Wade, *Louisiana Law Review*, vol. 21 (1960), p. 131.

11. Ibid., pp. 132–135.

12. MacIver, "The Social Significance of Professional Ethics," reprinted in *Professional Responsibility*, edited by M. Pirsig and K. Kirwin (St. Paul: West Publishing Co., 1976), p. 12. White and Wooten expand this idea by identifying a constellation of factors that contribute to the development of a specialized ethics for any professional group. Among these are the "values, norms, science, and laws existing within a given discipline." (Louis P. White and Kevin C. Wooten, *Professional Ethics and Practice in Organizational Development* [New York: Praeger Publishers, 1986], p. 74.) While they acknowledge that these factors may be influenced by the general ethics of society (p. 68), they emphasize that "professional ethics is clearly a specialized form of ethics" and that, historically, "there has been a lack of differentiation from other forms of ethics." (p. 72.)

13. Virginia Held, "The Division of Moral Labor and the Role of the Lawyer," in *The Good Lawyer*, edited by David Luban (Totowa, N.J.: Rowman & Allanheld, 1983), pp. 66–67.

14. R. M. Veatch, "Medical Ethics: Professional or Universal?" *Harvard Theological Review*, vol. 65 (1972), pp. 531–551. R. S. Downie concurs in "Professional Ethics: Further Comments," *Journal of Medical Ethics*, vol. 12 (December 1986), pp. 195–196. One theorist posits a form of rule utilitarianism that incorporates elements of virtue ethics as the general morality as the foundation of all ethics including professional ethics. See David James's

"What Is Professional Ethics?" *Philosophy Research Archieves*, vol. 10, Supplement, 1985.

15. Robert H. Aronson and Donald T. Weckstein, *Professional Responsibility* (St. Paul: West Publishing Co., 1980), p. 191.

16. MacIver, p. 12. A variation on the theme of the primacy of general ethics is in Thomas L. Shaefer's *Faith and the Professions* (Provo, Utah: Brigham Young University, 1987). Shaefer identifies the norms and values of the community as those that are meaningful for professional life. Indeed, we can learn about the community by attending to stories about good professionals: "There are three elements of the American community whose story is told as the story of a good doctor or good lawyer is told: family, church (religious congregation), and town." (p. 29.) Another theorist brings out that, even in a pluralistic society like America, there is sufficient moral consensus to provide the ground for professional ethics. (Paul F. Camenisch, *Grounding Professional Ethics in a Pluralistic Society* [New York: Haven Publications, 1983], p. 93.)

17. Veatch, p. 532.

18. Marvin E. Frankel, "The Search for Truth: An Umpirial View," *University of Pennsylvania Law Review*, vol. 123 (1975), pp. 1031–39.

19. "Bates v. State Bar of Arizona," *United States Supreme Court Reports*, vol. 43 (1977), p. 370.

20. ABA Reports, vol. 89 (1964), p. 381.

21. American Bar Association Commission on Evaluation of Professional Standards, *Model Rules of Professional Conduct (Proposed Final Draft)*, (American Bar Association, 1981), p. i.

22. Ibid.

23. Ibid., p. 25. See also documentation for how the codes of lawyers as well as for doctors and accountants have evolved in response to economic, social, and political factors in Jeanne F. Backof and Charles L. Martin, Jr., "Historical Perspectives: Development of Codes of Ethics in the Legal, Medical and Accounting Professions," *Journal of Business Ethics*, vol. 10, no. 2 (Fall 1991), pp. 99–110.

24. Monroe Friedman, "Professional Responsibility of the Criminal Defense Lawyer: The Three Hardest Questions," *Michigan Law Review*, vol. 64 (1966), p. 1469.

25. ABA, *Standards Relation to the Defense Function*, sec. 7. 7 Approved Draft (1971).

26. Ibid.

27. Norman Lefstein, "The Criminal Defendant Who Proposes Perjury," *Hofstra Law Review*, vol. 6, 1978, pp. 665–692, reprinted in *Ethics and the Legal Profession*, edited by Michael Davis and Frederick Elliston (Buffalo, N.Y.: Prometheus Books, 1986), p. 353.

28. *Model Code*, Disciplinary Rule 7-102 (B)(1).

29. *Model Rules*, Rule 3. 3.

30. "Nix v. Whiteside," *U. S. Reports*, vol. 475, 1986, reprinted in part in *Problems in Legal Ethics*, edited by M. Schwartz and R. Wydick (St. Paul: West Publishing Co., 1988), p. 172.

31. "ABA Commission on Ethics and Professional Responsibility," Formal Opinion #87-353, 1987.

32. *The Legal Profession: Responsibility and Regulation*, edited by Geoffrey C. Hazard, Jr., and Deborah R. Rhode (Westbury, N.Y.: The Foundation Press, Inc., 1988), p. 142.

33. Ibid., p. 238.

34. Ibid., p. 251.

35. Hazard, pp. 43–47.

36. See David Luban's initial introduction of the notion in his *Lawyers and Justice* (Princeton, N.J.: Princeton University Press, 1988), p. xxii.

37. E. D. Cohen, "Pure Legal Advocates and Moral Agents: Two Concepts of a Lawyer in an Adversary System," *Criminal Justice Ethics*, vol. 4, winter/spring, 1985, pp. 38–59.

38. American Bar Association, *Model Code of Professional Responsibility*(1980), p. 1 and American Bar Association, *Model Rules of Professional Conduct* (1983), p. 2.

39. *Model Code*, p. 21 and *Model Rules*, p. 6.

40. *Model Code*, p. 32 and *Model Rules*, p. 2.

41. *Model Code*, p. 21 and *Model Rules*, pp. 7, 8.

42. *Model Rules*, p. 2.

43. *Professional Responsibility*, edited by R. Aronson, J. Devine, and W. Fisch (St. Paul: West Publishing Co., 1985), pp. 511–653.

44. *The Lawyering Process: Ethics and Professional Responsibility*, edited by Gary Bellow and Bea Moulton (Mineola, N.Y.: The Foundation Press, Inc., 1981), pp. 89–231.

45. Ibid., p. 111.

46. Ibid., p. 122.

47. Philip B. Heymann and Lance Liebman, *The Social Responsibilities of Lawyers* (Westbury, N.Y.: The Foundation Press, Inc., 1988), p. 24.

48. Ibid.

49. *Cases and Materials on Professional Responsibilities of Lawyers*, edited by John F. Sutton, Jr. and John S. Dzienkowski (St. Paul: West Publishing Co., 1989), pp. 424–717.

50. *Becoming a Lawyer: A Humanistic Perspective on Legal Education and Professionalism*, edited by Elizabeth Dvorkin, Jack Himmelstein, and Howard Lesnick (St. Paul: West Publishing Co., 1981), pp. 1, 2.

51. Ibid., p. 175.

52. Ibid., p. 176.

53. Ibid., p. 127.

54. Edward H. Levi, *An Introduction to Legal Reasoning* (Chicago: The University of Chicago Press, 1949), pp. 24, 25. My aim at this point is to liken how lawyers deal with ethics to their treatment of law generally, with my ultimate goal being one of showing how legal ethics can serve as a model for general ethics. The underlying assumption is that moral reasoning has not been significantly similar to legal reasoning. But see Alan Goldman's "Legal Reasoning as a Model for Moral Reasoning." He brings out how some think that legal and moral reasoning are very different because of the principle of *stare decisis* in law. Goldman rejects this position and highlights the significance of consistency in both legal and moral reasoning. (*Law and Philosophy*, vol. 8 [April 1989], pp. 131–149.)

55. Ronald Dworkin, *Taking Rights Seriously* (Cambridge, Mass.: Harvard University Press, 1975), pp. 22–28.

56. Ronald Dworkin, *A Matter of Principle* (Cambridge, Mass.: Harvard University Press, 1985), p. 158.

57. Ibid., p. 159.

58. See Carol Gilligan, *In a Different Voice* (Cambridge, Mass.: Harvard University Press, 1982). Gilligan collaborated on a more recent work

that explores the ethics of care versus the justice approaches to morality and how the ethics of care approach is tied to a female perspective. See *Mapping the Moral Domain: A Contribution of Women's Thinking to Psychological Theory and Education*, edited by Carol Gilligan, Jamie Victoria Ward, and Jill McLean Taylor with Betty Bardige (Cambridge, Mass.: Center for the Study of Gender, Education, and Human Development, 1988).

59. Owen Flanagan, *Varieties of Moral Personality* (Cambridge, Mass.: Harvard University Press, 1991), p. 252. See also Richard Taylor's *Virtue Ethics* (Interlakan, N.Y.: Linden Books, 1991). Prof. Taylor laments the pre-occupation of contemporary ethicists with the correctness of human action and recommends that we follow the lead of ancient ethicists and concern ourselves with acquiring virtue, "the uncommonly good. "

60. Arthur Lovejoy, "The Thirteen Pragmatisms," *The Journal of Philosophy*, vol. 5, no. 8 (1908), pp. 36–39.

61. Israel Scheffler, "On Justification and Commitment," *Journal of Philosophy*, 1954, p. 183.

62. C. I. Lewis, *An Analysis of Knowledge and Valuation* (LaSalle, Ill.: Open Court, 1962), p. 3.

63. C. I. Lewis, *The Ground and Nature of the Right*(New York: Columbia University Press, 1955), p. 93.

64. C. I. Lewis, *Our Social Inheritance* (Bloomington, Ind.: Indiana University Press, 1957), p. 93.

65. C. I. Lewis, "Pragmatism and the Roots of the Moral," in *Values and Imperatives*, edited by John Lange (Stanford University Press, 1969), pp. 114–115.

66. John Dewey, *Ethics*, reprinted in *Intelligence in the Modern World*, edited by Joseph Tarner (New York: Random House, Inc., 1939), p. 777. Also, see, e. g., Dewey's *Theory of the Moral Life* (New York: Holt, Rinehart and Winston, 1960), *passim*.

67. William James, *Pragmatism* (New York: The World Publishing Company, 1907), p. 133.

68. Ibid.

69. Ibid.

70. Ibid.

CHAPTER 2

1. Leslie Stevenson, *Seven Theories of Human Nature* (Oxford, England: Clarendon Press, 1974), p. 3. For the best contemporary discussion of grounding a moral program in human nature, see Ija Lazari-Pawlowska's "Morality and Human Nature," *Dialectics and Humanism*, vol. 11, no. 1 (Winter 1984), pp. 213–216. Also, see a comment on this article in my "Human Nature and Ethical Standards," *Dialectics and Humanism*, vol. XVII, no. 1 (Winter 1990), pp. 102–106. See also Christopher Berry's *Human Nature* (Atlantic Highlands, N.J.: Humanities Press, 1986). Berry underlines the frequency with which human nature is involved and its essential role in political theorizing.

Owen Flanagan restates this prominent motif in ethical theory of "ought implies can" in his Principle of Minimal Psychological Realism: "Make sure when constructing a moral theory or projecting a moral ideal that the character, decision processing, and behavior prescribed are possible, or are perceived to be possible for creatures like us." Owen Flanagan, *Varieties of Moral Personality* [Cambridge, Mass.: Harvard University Press, 1991], p. 32.) He acknowledges that ethicists concern themselves with, and make claims about, human nature but "most ethicists pay no attention to the bearing on these claims of the exciting new work in psychology and the other human sciences." (p. vii.) His book is an attempt to inject this new work into moral philosophy, since "psychology matters deeply to moral philosophy." (p. 54.)

2. One might conceptualize these circumstances in a variety of ways. One might, for example, claim that, in effect, two senses of human nature are being employed. The first shows a human as some creature capable of structuring one's life in accord with some particular conception set out in the second sense, but, until one so structures it, one's identity as a human is primarily based on biological considerations and assessments of one's capabilities. The second sense suggests what it is to be fully human or truly human and shows the type of person one can become but which one is not to begin with, nor need one ever become. Alternatively, one might say that until one does, in fact, act in accord with some specified, reflective conception of human nature, one is not human at all, thus restricting "human nature" to the second sense above. One might also carve the pie in such a fashion that there is a single sense of human nature marked by stages, where it is only in the later stages that one attains one's full identity as a human and it always remains possible for one not to reach these later stages or to revert once one attains them. In any case, the main point is that, while there is some conception that a person qua human is to meet, one's doing so is not necessary. When one does meet this conception, however, one at once conforms to the ethical advice that humans should be following.

Kant seems to fit here in that he portrays humans as rational beings and indicates that consistency of action is a chief requirement for such beings. The categorical imperative, of course, directs us to act only according to that maxim which we can, at the same time, will to become universal law. In acting out of a sense of duty for this command, we are to set aside all other motives and inclinations. One does not necessarily act in this fashion. One may contribute to charity out of the generosity of one's heart; one may withhold a contribution because of one's niggardliness. Yet, when one does so, one falls short of performing as the rational being which one is or can be. Here again we have a situation where the human, acting in accord with a certain conception of what a human is, in effect, is subscribing to the advice that one should be acting in that manner although it is clear that one can, because of one's nature, fall short of this demand. Epicurus seems to fit here, too, insofar as he suggests that we should pare down and, if possible, eliminate our desires and appetites so that we might experience the highest pleasure, *ataraxia*, a peaceful state of mind where one experiences a freedom from his desires. To be sure we can act otherwise as do the lower pleasure seekers that Epicurus condemns.

One commentator describes such approaches to tying human nature to ethical theory as teleological in that they incorporate what we are with what we ought to become. Concerned with the arbitrariness associated with projects attempting to establish our "true end," Eggerman suggests that we confine ourselves to "the concept of factual human nature" in ethics. ("Is the Concept of 'Human Nature' Indispensable to Ethics?" in *Contemporary Essays on Greek Ideas: The Kilgore Festschrift*, edited by Robert M. Baird et al. [Waco, Texas: Baylor University Press, 1987], pp. 127–140.)

3. Jeremy Bentham, *The Principles of Morals and Legislation* (New York: Hafner Publishing Co., 1948), p. 1.

4. Robin Attfield, "On Being Human," *Inquiry*, vol. 17 (1974), pp. 181–184.

5. George G. Marshall, "Human Nature Changes," *The New Scholasticism*, vol. 54, no. 2 (1980), p. 170.

6. J. K. Feibleman, "Technology and Human Nature," *Southwestern Journal of Philosophy*, vol. 10 (Spring 1979), pp. 35–41.

7. A. S. Cua, "Morality and Human Nature," *Philosophy East and West*, vol. 32 (July 1982), p. 279.

8. Ibid., pp. 287–288.

9. Janna L. Thompson, "Mutual Aid and Selfish Genes," *Metaphilosophy*, vol. 15, nos. 3 & 4 (July/October 1984), p. 279.

10. Cua, p. 287.

11. Thompson, pp. 279–280.

12. Milton Fisk, "The Human Nature Argument," *Social Praxis*, vol. 5, 1978, p. 360.

13. George Herbert Mead, *Mind, Self, and Society*, edited by Charles W. Morris (Chicago: University of Chicago Press, 1934), p. 135. See how Michael L. Schwalbe draws on Mead's views in his discussion of role theory and the social self in "Mead Among the Cognitivists: Role as Performance Imagery," *Journal of the Theory of Social Behavior*, vol. 17 (June 1987), pp. 113–133.

14. Erich Fromm and Ramon Xirau, "Introduction," in *The Nature of Man*, edited, with introduction, by Fromm and Xirau (New York: The Macmillan Company, 1968), p. 3.

15. Ibid.

16. Tenets of major religions presented were gleaned from entries in *The Encyclopedia of Philosophy* (New York: Macmillan Publishing Co., Inc. & The Free Press, 1967), including "Hinduism," pp. 1–4 of vol. 4; "Jainism," pp. 238–239 of vol. 4; "Buddhism," pp. 416–420 of vol. 1; and "Christianity," pp. 104–108 of vol. 2.

17. Jean-Paul Sartre, *Nausea*, translated by Lloyd Alexander (New York: New Directions Publishing Corporation, 1964), p. 237.

18. Ibid., p. 237. In trying to account for the origin of a modern theory of human nature like Sartre's, Peter Langford considers the possibility that the new, psychoanalytic method that Sartre employed allowed Sartre to deliver up his theory. Langford rejects that possibility and argues for the historical decline of Christianity as a more likely possibility. Peter Langford, *Modern Philosophies of Human Nature* (Boston: Martinus Nijhoff Publishers, 1986), p. 215.

19. Herman Hesse, *Steppenwolf*, translated by Basil Creighton (New York: Holt, Rinehart, and Winston, 1963), p. 218.

20. Ibid., p. 218.

21. Ibid., p. 219.

22. Ibid., p. 220.

23. Lawrence Kohlberg, "Education for Justice: A Modern Statement of the Platonic View," in *Five Lectures on Moral Education* (Cambridge, Mass.: Harvard University Press, 1970), pp. 71–72. See Kohlberg's collabo-

rative effort with Anne Colby, John Gibbs, and Marcus Lieberman to document his theory of development. (*A Longitudinal Study of Moral Judgment* [Chicago: Society for Research in Child Development, Inc., 1983].)

24. Jean Piaget, *The Moral Judgment of the Child*, translated by Marjorie Gabain (Glencoe, Ill.: The Free Press, 1932), p. 17.

25. Ibid., p. 17.

26. Ibid., p. 18.

27. Ibid., pp. 17–18.

28. See, e. g., Immanuel Kant's *Foundations of the Methaphysics of Morals*, translated by Lewis White Beck (New York: The Bobbs-Merrill Company, Inc., 1959).

29. John Lange, "The Late Papers of C. I. Lewis," *Journal of the History of Philosophy*, vol. 14, no. 3 (1966), p. 235.

30. See, e. g., C. I. Lewis's "Pragmatism and the Roots of the Moral," in *Values and Imperatives*, edited by John Lange (Stanford, Calif.: Stanford University Press, 1969), p. 118. See also, for a complete statement of the position, Lewis's *An Analysis of Knowledge and Valuation* (La Salle: Open Court, 1962).

31. Lewis, "Pragmatism and the Roots of the Moral," p. 120.

32. Ibid.

33. See, e. g., Lewis's "An Attempted Answer," in *Values and Imperatives*, p. 66.

34. Richard Taylor, *Good and Evil* (London: The Macmillan Co., 1970), pp. 13–14.

35. Robert McShea, "Human Nature Ethical Theory," *Philosophy and Phenomenological Research*, vol. 39 (March 1979), p. 387.

36. Florian von Schilcher and Neil Tennant, *Philosophy, Evolution, and Human Nature* (Boston: Routledge & Kegan Paul, 1984), p. 163. See also Alexander Rosenberg's attempt to limit the application of biology to ethics. He claims that biological theory might help us to understand why cooperation emerged as a necessary condition for morality. (Alexander Rosenberg, "The Biological Justification of Ethics," *Social Philosophy and Policy*, vol. 8, no. 1 [Autumn 1990], pp. 86–101.) Roger Trigg opts for our understanding people with both cultural and biological accounts and warns against invoking either account in the absence of the other. ("The Sociobiological View of Man," *Philosophy*, Supplement, 1984, pp. 93–110.) William Grey tries to

account for why we are content to substitute causal for teleological explanations in physics but not in biology in "Evolution and the Meaning of Life," *Zygon*, vol. 22 (December 1987), pp. 479–496.

37. Role theoretical research following Pleck's theory of "role overload" is concerned with how people respond when the demands of a role become too great. People usually choose ways to reduce the overload that bring the greatest relief. Applying this terminology to our case at hand, we could describe the phenomenon of seeing ourselves in conflicting ways as contributing to the tension of overload that needs to be relieved. See M. Van Vonderen's "Role Theory: A Reconstruction," *Methodology and Science*, vol. 22, no. 3 (1989), pp. 168–177.

38. Other theorists similarly invite us to think more broadly about the competing claims upon the professional's conduct. Arleen Dallery, for example, in calling for an "ethics of participation," asserts, "The question is not what ought I to do but of what histories am I part? What kind of action or course of action is involved in joining collective projects, subscribing to codes, associating with peers, associating with outsiders?" ("Professional Loyalties," *The Applied Turn in Contemporary Philosophy*, Bowling Green Studies in Applied Philosophy, vol. 5 [1983], p. 83.) But while such theorists see the loyalties stemming from our varying roles as many and sometimes conflicting, they present these loyalties and roles as givens. Others, like Gerald Postema, agree that professionals should integrate their professional role activities with those outside the role but introduce some flexibility in the role. Postema speaks of a "recourse role" where "one's duties and responsibilities are not fixed, but may expand or contract depending on the institutional objectives the role is designed to serve." ("Moral Responsibility in Professional Ethics," *Profits and Professions* [Clifton, N.J.: Humana Press, 1983], p. 53.) My view calls for the agent's actively constructing conceptions of roles as well as for the agent harmonizing the demands of these roles in his or her person.

39. Lon Fuller, *The Law in Quest of Itself* (Chicago: The Foundation Press, Inc., 1940).

CHAPTER 3

1. Donald T. Weckstein, "Training for Professionalism," *Connecticut Law Review*, vol. 4 (1972), p. 412.

2. Roscoe Pound, *The Lawyer from Antiquity to Modern Times* (St. Paul: West Publishing Co., 1953), p. 6.

3. Peter Wright, "What Is a Profession?" *Canadian Bar Review*, vol. 29 (1951), p. 757.

4. Wilbert Moore, *The Professions: Roles and Rules* (New York: Russell Sage Foundation, 1970), p. 4.

5. John B. Cullen, *The Structure of Professionalism* (New York: Petrocelli Books, Inc., 1978). Consider also Thomas Schaefer's insight that, although it may be difficult to define professionalism, it is much like honesty in that we know it when we see it. ("Professionalism: Foundation for Business Ethics," *Journal of Business Ethics*, vol. 3 [November 1984], pp. 269–278.)

6. Elliot Freidson, "Professions and the Occupational Principle," in *The Professions and their Prospects*," edited by Elliot Freidson (Beverly Hills, Calif.: Sage Publications, 1973), p. 19.

7. Ronald Pavalko, *Sociology of Occupations and Professions* (Itasca, Ill.: F. E. Peacock Publishers, Inc., 1971), p. vii. One commentator brings out how the concern of sociologists with the characteristics of professions is descriptive as against the decidedly evaluative concern of the philosopher. This concern prompts us to inquire into what is essential to professions that allows them to function in a unique and socially valuable fashion. (R. S. Downie, "Professions and Professionalism," *Journal of Philosophy of Education*, vol. 24, no. 2 (Winter 1990), pp. 147–159.)

Other comments on the literature draw our attention to there not yet being any "absolute agreement on the definition of the 'profession,'" given that "theoretical and methodological consensus is not yet so great among sociologists." (Bernard Barber, "Some Problems in the Sociology of the Professions," in *The Professions in America*, edited by Kenneth S. Lynn and the Editors of *Daedalus* [Boston: Beacon Press, 1965], p. 17.) But still others wish to codify precisely the nature of the consensus that has been reached, being particularly motivated, it seems, to distill the vast literature, and also account for the consensus by appealing to the magnitude of the writings on the topic: "There has developed an extensive body of literature dealing with the characteristics of 'professions.' This body of research and writing includes a wide variety of material, ranging from historical analyses of the development of particular occupations to case studies of the status of specific work activities as professions.... Work on this topic has become so voluminous that substantial consensus has emerged on these dimensions and it is possible to identify key features of work groups that appear to occur in combinations and clusters that function to differentiate 'occupations' from 'professions.'" (Ronald Pavalko, *Sociology of Occupations and Professions*, pp. 15–16.)

8. Some recent discussions of roles include those by Bernard Williams, Alan H. Goldman, and David Luban. See Williams's "Goodness

and Roles," in *Morality: An Introduction to Ethics* (New York: Harper and Row, 1972), pp. 51–58. See Goldman's *The Moral Foundations of Professional Ethics* (Totowa, N.J.: Rowman and Littlefield, 1980), pp. 20–33. And see Luban's *Lawyers and Justice* (Princeton, N.J.: Princeton University Press, 1988), pp. 104–147, The *locus classicus* on roles, of course, is F. H. Bradley's *Ethical Studies* (Oxford, England: Oxford University Press, 1927). Margaret Coyne makes a good point about how roles can dictate arational acts and are thereby in need of moral critique. This is the very point I wish to make using the ideas of nonreflective and partially reflective attitudes toward roles as arational or nearly so in contrast to the critical attitude. See Coyne's "Role and Rational Action," in *Journal of the Theory of Social Behavior*, vol. 14 (1984), pp. 259–276.

9. Michael Bayles, *Professional Ethics* (Belmont, Mass.: Wadsworth Publishing Company, 1981), p. 7.

10. Ernest Greenwood, "The Elements of Professionalization," in *Professionalization*, edited by H. Vollmer and D. Mills (Englewood Cliffs, N.J.: Prentice Hall, Inc., 1966), pp. 10–11.

11. Bernard Barber, "Some Problems in the Sociology of the Professions," in *The Professions in America*, edited by Kenneth S. Lynn and the Editors of *Daedalus* (Boston: Beacon Press, 1965), pp. 18–19.

12. Ibid., p. 19.

13. Ibid., p. 17.

14. John B. Cullen, *The Structure of Professionalism* (New York: Petrocelli Books, Inc., 1978), pp. 1–2.

15. Ibid., p. 2.

16. Ibid., p. 2.

17. Ibid., p. 2.

18. "Professional Responsibility: Report of the Joint Conference," in *American Bar Association Journal*, vol. 44 (1958), p. 1159.

19. *Selected Readings on the Legal Profession*, edited, with introductions, by Benjamin F. Boyer, Albert J. Harno, and Robert E. Mathews (St. Paul: West Publishing Co., 1962), p. 4. Although it is clear from this quotation that some thinkers see the knowledge component of a profession as having moral implications and thus being intimately connected, others see knowledge and ethics vying with each other for the central feature of a profession. See Michael Davis, *"The Special Role of Professions in Business Ethics Journal*, vol. 7, no. 2 (Summer 1988), pp. 51–62. Camenisch makes a

broader case for professions having duties to serve public interest. He argues that professions are moral subcommunities of society and, as such, should ground their ethics in the values of society and assist society in achieving what it values. See Paul F. Camenisch, *Grounding Professional Ethics in a Pluralistic Society* (New York: Haven Publications, 1983), especially pp. 93, 115, 130, 135.

20. Alan Soble, "Some Remarks on Professionalism," in *Business and Professional Ethics*, vol. 1, no. 3 (1978), p. 10.

21. Robert J. Herrick, "Further Remarks on Professionalism," in *Business and Professional Ethics*, vol. 1, no. 4 (1978), p. 2.

22. James Jackson, "Law and Lawyers," in *The Legal Mind in America*, edited by Perry Miller (Ithaca, N.Y.: Cornell University Press, 1962), p. 277.

23. Peter Wright, "What Is a Profession," in *Canadian for Review*, vol. 29 (1951), p. 757.

24. Pound, p. 8.

25. Ibid., p. 9.

26. Ernest Greenwood, "The Elements of Professionalization," in *Professionalization*, edited by Howard M. Vollmer and Donald L. Mills (Englewood Cliffs, N.J.: Prentice-Hall, Inc., 1966), p. 10.

27. Ibid., p. 11.

28. Everett C. Hughes, "Professions," in *The Professions in America*, edited by Kenneth S. Lynn and the Editors of Daedalus (Boston: Beacon Press, 1965), p. 6. For a discussion of the important role that the imagination plays in mediating between the general and the particular and of the significance of that mediating in the practice of law, see Anthony Kronman's "Practical Wisdom and Professional Character," in *Social Philosophy and Politics*, vol. 4 (Autumn 1986), pp. 203–234.

29. A. N. Whitehead, *Adventures of Ideas* (New York: The Macmillan Company, 1956), pp. 72–73.

30. *Discussion Draft, A. B. A. Model Rules of Professional Conduct* (Chicago: The American Bar Association, 1980), p. 2.

31. John W. Wade, "Public Responsibilities of the Learned Professions," in *Louisiana Law Review*, vol. 21 (1960), pp. 130–131.

32. A. M. Carr-Saunders, "Professionalization in Historical Perspective," in *Professionalization*, edited by Howard M. Vollmer and Donald L. Mills (Englewood Cliffs, N.J.: Prentice-Hall, Inc., 1966), pp. 7–8.

33. Pound, pp. 4–5.

34. Ibid., p. 5.

35. Ibid., pp. 9–10.

36. See, e. g., F. Raymond Marks's *The Lawyer, The Public, and Professional Responsibility* (Chicago: American Bar Foundation, 1972), pp. 248–249. One commentator points to how financial and social pressures on the lawyer to succeed can put the attorney in a situation where interests conflict; the attorney may be tempted to provide unnecessary service when clients query whether they need services. Assuming this scenario to be plausible, we see further evidence of how the traditional motive of practicing for public service becomes eroded. See Banks McDowell, "The Professional's Dilemma: Choosing between Service and Success," in *Business and Professional Ethics Journal*, vol. 9, nos. 1–2 (Spring–Summer 1990), pp. 35–52. See also the reminder to the medical profession of the essential link between service and the professions and the call to pay more attention to the ideal of service. (Allan R. Dyer, "Ethics, Advertising, and the Definition of a Profession," in *Journal of Medical Ethics*, vol. 11 (June 1985), pp. 72–78. Shannon L. Jung brings out how commercialization exacerbates the fashion in which the ideal of service is eroded by professionals striving for personal gain and investigates ways to harmonize the two in "Commercialization and the Professions," in *Business and Professional Ethics Journal*, vol. 2 (Winter 1983), pp. 57–82. Frederic G. Reamer calls upon social workers qua professionals to reinstate their preoccupation with public welfare in "Social Work: Calling or Career?" *Hastings Center Report* Supp. 17 (Fall 1987), pp. 14–15.

37. Bernard Barber, "Some Problems in the Sociology of the Professions," in *The Professions in America*, pp. 18–19.

38. Greenwood, pp. 16–17.

39. Ibid., p. 12.

40. William Goode, "The Librarian: From Occupation to Profession?" in *Professionalization*, p. 42.

41. Hughes, p. 3. Richard Wasserstrom acknowledges that lawyers and their clients may well be in an unequal relationship as regards knowledge. But typically this inequality is attended by manipulative and paternalistic actions of attorneys and is thereby criticizable. See his "Lawyers as Professionals: Some Moral Issues," in *Human Rights Quarterly*, vol. 5, no. 1 (1975), pp. 105–128.

42. Thomas S. Szasz and Marc H. Hollender, "The Basic Models of the Doctor–Patient Relationship," *A. M. A. Archieves of Internal Medicine*, vol. 97 (1956), pp. 585–592.

43. Robert M. Veatch, "Models for Ethical Medicine in a Revolutionary Age," in *Hastings Center Report*, vol. 2 (June 1972), pp. 5–7. Before positing the fiduciary model, yet another alternative to the paternalistic model, Joseph Ellis offers an inventory of the many conceptions governing the doctor-patient relationship in "Lying and Deception: The Solution to a Dilemma in Medical Ethics," in *Westminster Institute Review*, vol. 1, May 1981, pp. 3–6. And Mary Mahowald argues for substituting paternalism with parentalism or the professional's use of power to give power to others. See her "Power and Professional Life," in *Philosophical Essays*, edited by Yeager Hudson (Lewiston, Maine: Mellen Press, 1988), pp. 257–269. For a discussion of the patient's obligations on the contract model, see Martin Benjamin's "Lay Obligations in Professional Relations," in *Journal of Medical Philosophy*, vol. 10 (1985), pp. 85–103.

44. Pound, p. 361. See also how Bruce Kimball aligns one's having final authority in making decisions with one's being a professional. He argues that, given current federal and state regulations, teachers lack such authority and thus cannot be considered professionals. (Bruce A. Kimball, "The Problems of Teachers' Authority in the Light of the Structural Analysis of Professions," in *Educational Theory*, vol. 38 [Winter 1988], pp. 1–9.)

45. See, e. g., C. I. Lewis's "The Meaning of Liberty," in *Values and Imperatives*, edited by John Lange (Stanford, Calif.: Stanford University Press, 1969).

46. Everett C. Hughes, "The Social Context of Professionalism," in *Professionalization*, p. 69.

47. James Adams, "The Social Import of the Professions," in *Selected Readings on the Legal Profession*, p. 74. See the similar point here that professionals should interpret society's values and assist in harmonizing those that conflict in Bruce Jennings, D. Callahan, and S. Wolf's "The Professions: Public Interest and Common Good," in *Hastings Center Report Supp.*, 17 (Fall 1987), pp. 3–10. But consider Hauptman and Hill's opposing view that professionals are largely responsible for American society's ethics diminishing. (Robert Hauptman and Fred Hill, "Deride, Abide, or Dissent: On the Ethics of Professional Conduct," in *Journal of Business Ethics*, vol. 10, no. 1 (January 1991), pp. 37–44.

48. Robert Schultz, "On the Meaning and Value of Professionalism," unpublished manuscript, p. 17. Prof. Schultz, now at University of Washington, Bothell Branch, delivered this paper at Calgary University's Summer Institute on Professionalism.

49. Robert M. Veatch, "Medical Ethics: Professional or Universal?" in *Harvard Theological Review*, vol. 65 (1972), p. 532.

50. Weckstein, pp. 412–414. Behrman concurs with this assessment of the average person's inability to evaluate professional activity but admonishes that unless professionals regulate themselves, society will regulate professionals with "increasingly severe constraints." Because of the importance of a profession's enforcing its code to maintain its autonomy, Behrman lists "surveillance" as a separate feature of a profession. (Jack N. Behrman, *Essays on Ethics in Business and the Professions* [Englewood Cliffs, N.J.: Prentice Hall, 1988], p. 102.)

Lisa Newton identifies a code of ethics as essential for a profession. She thinks a code's significance follows from a necessary fact of social existence—a social contract—wherein professions ensure, with their codes, that vital services will be provided in exchange for favorable treatment in the marketplace. Or, it can be seen as following from the nature of professional standards that are vehicles for memorializing the guiding ideal of professional service. See Newton's "Lawgiving for Professional Life: Reflections on the Place of the Professional Code," in *Business and Professional Ethics Journal* (Fall 1981), pp. 41–53.

51. Adams, pp. 73–74. One commentator suggests that we should think of codes of ethics as unique to professions and brings out how in a calling that is not a profession, like the discipline of philosophy, a code of ethics is not appropriate. (D. G. Brown, "On Professing to be a Profession," in *Dialogue* [Canada], vol. 25 [Winter 1986], pp. 753–756.)

52. Moore, pp. 119–120.

53. Carr-Saunders, pp. 4–5.

54. Ibid., pp. 5–6. In 1984 the *Business and Professional Ethics Journal* featured a debate on the function of professional associations and codes and on who should be overseeing the activities of professionals—whether professionals themselves can do so or whether governmental overseeing is in order. See *Business and Professional Ethics Journal*, vol. 3 (Winter 1984), pp. 43–68 (including contributions by J. W. Snapper, M. Lunch, D. Wilson, and J. Ladd).

55. Paul Freund, "The Legal Profession," in *The Professions in America*, p. 38.

56. Ibid.

57. Ibid.

58. S. M. Lipset and M. A. Schwartz, "The Politics of Professionals," in *Professionalization*, edited by H. Vollmer and D. Mills (Englewood Cliffs, N.J.: Prentice-Hall, Inc., 1966), p. 299.

59. Henry S. Drinker, *Legal Ethics* (Westport, Conn.: Greenwood Press, 1953), p. xii.

60. Ibid.

61. Ibid., p. xiii.

62. Ibid.

63. Richard Rush, *American Jurisprudence*, passages reprinted in *The Legal Mind in America*, p. 47.

64. Drinker, p. 5.

65. Marks, pp. 248–249.

66. Ibid., p. 246.

67. Pound, p. xxviii.

68. Ibid., p. 232.

69. Ibid., p. xxvii.

70. Ibid., pp. 10–11. But consider Michael Bayles's thesis that although professionals might best be left to regulate themselves on technical matters, nonprofessionals should regulate professionals on the nontechnical. (Michael Bayles, "Professional Power and Self-Regulation," in *Business and Professional Ethics Journal*, vol. 5 [1986], pp. 26–46.)

71. Ibid., p. xxiv.

72. Drinker, p. 7.

73. Ibid., p. 7.

74. Pound, p. xxvi.

75. Rush, p. 44.

76. See, e. g., "Plain Language Update," in *Americans for Legal Reform*, vol. 2 (1981), p. 6.

77. "Bates v. State Bar of Arizona," in *United States Supreme Court Reports*, vol. 43 (1977), p. 370.

78. Charles Fried, *Right and Wrong* (Cambridge, Mass.: Harvard University Press, 1978), p. 190. M. B. E. Smith draws attention to the recent efforts of philosophers to demonstrate how lawyers' roles can lead lawyers to moral wrongdoing and bad character. He offers a negative answer to the question he raises in "Should Lawyers Listen to Philosophers about Legal Ethics," in *Law and Philosophy*, vol. 9, no. 1 (Fall 1990), pp. 67–93.

79. "Bates," p. 371.

80. Fried, p. 192.

CHAPTER 4

1. Stephen Landsman, *The Adversary System, A Description and a Defense* (Washington, D.C.: American Enterprise Institute for Public Policy Research, 1984), p. 2.

2. G. C. Hazard, Jr., *Ethics in the Practice of Law* (New Haven, Conn.: Yale University Press, 1978), p. 120.

3. Lon L. Fuller, "The Forms and Limits of Adjudication," in *Harvard Law Review*, vol. 92, no. 2 (1978), p. 364.

4. Ibid.

5. Ibid., p. 365.

6. Lon L. Fuller, "The Adversary System," in *Talks on American Law*, edited by Harold Berman (New York: Random House, 1961), pp. 34–35.

7. Landsman, p. 1.

8. Ibid., p. 4.

9. Ibid., pp. 4–5.

10. Dean McCormick, *Handbook of the Law of Evidence*, second edition (St. Paul: West Publishing Co., 1972), p. 12.

11. Ibid., p. 12.

12. Ibid., p. 13.

13. Ibid., pp. 13–14.

14. Hazard, p. 120.

15. Ibid.

16. Ibid.

17. Ibid., pp. 121–122.

18. Raymond A. Belliotti, "Values in the Courtroom: Two Kinds of Judicial Systems," in *Westminster Institute Review*, vol. 1, no. 3 (1981), p. 3.

19. Monroe H. Freedman, "Lawyer and Client: Personal Responsibility in a Professional System," in *Ethics and Advocacy* (Sponsored by the Roscoe Pound—American Trial Lawyers Foundation, 1978), p. 61. Freedman tells us he is drawing on language from Rifkind, a well-known advocate.

20. Ibid., p. 3.

21. L. Ray Patterson and Elliot E. Cheatham, *The Profession of Law* (Mineola, N.Y.: The Foundation Press, Inc., 1971), p. 82.

22. Ibid., p. 84.

23. Ibid., p. 85.

24. Freedman, p. 61.

25. F. Raymond Marks, et al., *The Professional Lawyer, the Public, and Professional Responsibility* (Chicago: American Bar Foundation, 1972), p. 9.

26. Ibid., p. 10.

27. Ibid.

28. Robert J. Kutak, "The Adversary System and the Practice of Law," in *The Good Laywer*, edited by David Luban (Totowa, N.J.: Rowman & Allanheld: 1984), p. 173.

29. Ibid., p. 174.

30. American Bar Association, *Model Code of Professional Responsibility* (Chicago: National Center for Professional Responsibility, 1980), pp. 32 and 34; *Model Rules of Professional Conduct* (1983), pp. 2 and 5.

31. "The Zealous Lawyer: Is Winning the Only Thing?" *QQ–Report from the Center for Philosophy and Public Policy*, vol. 4, no. 1 (1984), p. 1.

32. Marvin E. Frankel, "The Search for Truth: An Umpireal View," in *University of Pennsylvania Law Review*, vol. 123 (1975), p. 1032.

33. Jethro K. Lieberman, *Crisis at the Bar* (New York: W. W. Norton & Co., Inc., 1978), p. 51.

34. Lord Brougham, "Trial of Queen Caroline," in *J. Nightingale*, vol. 2 (1821), p. 8.

35. Alan H. Goldman, *The Moral Foundations of Professional Ethics* (Totowa, N.J.: Roman and Littlefield, 1980), p. 90.

36. Landsman, p. 5.

37. Ibid.

38. Fuller, p. 384.

39. Ibid., p. 384.

40. Ibid., p. 357.

41. Ibid.

42. Ibid., p. 363.

43. Ibid., p. 366.

44. Lieberman, p. 52. Consider also the view that the adversary system, together with laissez-faire capitalism and political pluralism in America, all have as their foundation a view of humans as basically self-interested and competitive by nature. Paul T. Wangerin, "Role Differentiation Problems in Professional Ethics," in *Business and Professional Ethics Journal*, vol. 9, nos. 1–2 (Spring–Summer 1990), pp. 171–180.

45. Ibid.

46. Belliotti, p. 3.

47. Ibid.

48. Kutak, p. 174.

49. Ibid.

50. Ibid., p. 175

51. Alan Donagan, "Justifying Legal Practice in the Adversary System," in *The Good Lawyer*, p. 124.

52. Belliotti, p. 4.

53. Goldman, p. 98.

54. Ann Strick, *Injustice for All* (New York: G. P. Putnam's Sons, 1977), p. 20.

55. Landsman, p. 45 and Fuller, p. 383.

56. Landsman, p. 45.

57. Ibid., p. 44.

58. "The Zealous Lawyer: Is Winning the Only Thing?" p. 2.

59. Landsman, p. 44.

60. Ibid.

61. Donagan, p. 124.

62. Belliotti, p. 3.

63. Hazard, p. 129.

64. J. R. Lucas, *On Justice* (Oxford, England: Clarendon Press, 1980), p. 87.

65. Landsman, p. 47.

66. Freedman, p. 60.

67. Hazard, p. 123.

68. Fuller, p. 384.

69. Landsman, pp. 49–50, and Hazard, p. 121.

70. "The Zealous Lawyer," p. 2.

71. Frankel, p. 21.

72. Goldman, p. 137.

73. Lucas, p. 88.

74. "The Zealous Lawyer," p. 2. For an analysis of the significance of each side's not being equally balanced, see Alan Wertheimer's "The Equalization of Legal Resources," in *Philosophy and Public Affairs*, vol. 17 (Fall 1988), pp. 303–322. Wertheimer argues that there is reason to equalize resources if the evidence shows that superior resources cause injustices that could be reduced if the resources where equalized.

75. Graham Hughes, "A Mixed Bane," Review of Phillip M. Stern's *Lawyers on Trial, The New York Review of Books*, March 19, 1981, p. 16.

76. Ibid.

77. Lieberman, p. 170.

78. Lucas, pp. 88–89.

79. Derek C. Bok, "A Flawed System," in *Harvard Magazine*, May–June 1983, p. 45.

80. Strick, p. 105.

81. Belliotti, p. 3.

82. Owen Flanagan also rejects any idea of the agent's environment being fixed and explores the causal connection between environment or context and behavior. He mentions some experiments that suggest that people in a hurry are less likely to assist others in need then people who are not in a hurry. He brings out how we can manipulate the environment with this knowledge to promote moral conduct. (Owen Flanagan, *Varieties of Moral Personality* [Cambridge, Mass.: Harvard University Press, 1991], pp. 293–332.)

CHAPTER 5

1. For a similar integrative methodology see *Act and Agent: Philosophical Foundations For Moral Education and Character Development*, edited by George F. McLean et al. (New York: University Press of America, 1986). Urged here is "coordinated contributions from ethics, developmental psychology, and education, designed to complement, enrich and promote existing moral education approaches." (p. 2.)

2. Robertson Davies, *Fifth Business* (New York: The Viking Press, 1970). Owen Flanagan opens his book with a discussion of saints and observes how they do not adhere to some all-encompassing ethical principle or display every good quality. He finds this observation significant for a couple of reasons. For one thing it suggests the poverty of the notion of the necessity of average moral agents aspiring to follow a single rule or to acquire all of some fixed set of qualities. For another, it has us search for an adequate psychology that accounts both for gaps in people's moral development and for the wide range of moral personalities. (Owen Flanagan, *Varieties of Moral Personality* [Cambridge, Mass.: Harvard University Press, 1991], pp. 1–12.) See John Silber's discussion of the importance of exemplars and heroes in our lives in his "Of Mermaids and Magnificance," in *Bostonia*, vol. 60. no. 3 (October 1986), pp. 18–21 and p. 50.

3. Plato, *Meno*, Steph., p. 73.

4. Ibid., Steph., p. 100.

5. Ibid., Steph., p. 1.

6. Ibid., Steph., p. 2–87.

7. Aristotle, *Nicomachean Ethics in Introduction to Aristotle*, edited by Richard McKeon, (New York: Random House, 1947), p. 340.

8. Ibid., p. 341.

9. Ibid., p. 347. See Thomas E. Schaefer's Aristotelian approach to becoming a professional. He brings out how practitioners of professionalism learn professionalism by practicing it. ("Professionalism: Foundation for Business Ethics," in *Journal of Business Ethics*, vol. 3 [November 1984], pp. 269–278.)

10. Lawrence Kohlberg, "Education for Justice: A Modern Statement of the Platonic View," in *Moral Education, Five Lectures*, edited by Nancy F. Sizer and Theodore R. Sizer (Cambridge, Mass.: Harvard University Press, 1970), p. 63.

11. Ibid., p. 69.

12. Ibid., pp. 70–77.

13. William K. Frankena, "Toward a Philosophy of Moral Education," *Harvard Educational Review*, vol. 28, no. 4 (Fall 1958), pp. 302–304, 308–311.

14. R. S. Peters, "Reason and Habit," *The Education in a Changing Society*, edited by W. R. Nibet (London: Faber & Faber Ltd., 1963) pp. 46–65.

15. While I have made no claim to have shown that role modeling is a feature of all theories of moral education, I can here suggest how some other theories of moral education not mentioned in the main text can be seen as employing a hypothesis of role modeling. William Hare brings out how such contemporary approaches to moral education as values clarification and situational ethics stress open-mindedness in an attempt to eschew both indoctrination and an emphasis on absolute moral rules. In these cases, we can see the open-minded agent as the role model. See Hare's "Open-mindedness in Moral Education," in *Journal of Moral Education*, vol. 16 (May 1987), pp. 99–107. Other recent approaches to moral education, like Gilligan's ethics of care, can be seen as establishing as a role model an agent oriented towards caring for others and interested in developing interpersonal relations.

16. Albert Bandura, "Analysis of Modeling Process," in *Psychological Modeling* (Chicago: Aldine, Atherton, 1971), p. 1.

17. Ibid., pp. 1–2.

18. Ibid., and Albert Bandura, *Social Learning Theory* (Englewood Cliffs, N.J.: Prentice-Hall, Inc., 1977), pp. 24–25 See Thomas L. Schaefer's *Faith and the Professions* (Provo, Utah: Brigham Young University, 1987). Schaefer brings out that when stories portray doctors and lawyers as "attractive in a morally influential formative way" (p. 21), they, in effect,

depict "acts of character in community" and include the qualities of "being compelling, being prodigious, being in touch with the numinous, being useful, and being a thinker." (p. 28.) Schaefer argues for teaching professional ethics by attending to stories that depict such heroes.

19. Bandura, *Social Learning Theory*, p. 25, and Bandura, "Analysis," p. 39.

20. Bandura, *Social Learning Theory*, p. 17.

21. Ibid., p. 12.

22. Ibid., p. 12 and 22, and Bandura, "Analysis," pp. 2–3.

23. Bandura, *Social Learning Theory*, p. 17.

24. Ibid., p. vii, and Bandura "Analysis" p. 16.

25. Bandura, *Social Learning Theory*, p. 10.

26. Bandura, "Analysis," p. 2.

27. Ibid., pp. 1–2, 4–5 and Bandura, "Analysis," pp. 3–4.

28. See Gabriel Tarde, *The Laws of Imitation* (New York: Holt, Reinhart, and Winston, 1903).

29. See N. E. Miller and J. Dollard, *Social Learning and Justification* (New Haven, Conn.: Yale University Press, 1941).

30. See J. Piaget, *Plays, Dreams and Imitation in Childhood* (New York: Norton, 1951).

31. Bandura, *Social Learning Theory*, p. 13.

32. Bandura, "Analysis," p. 39.

33. Ibid., p. 35.

34. Ibid., p. 37.

INDEX

▼

Adversary system: alternatives for conceiving of, 63–64, 112–129; based on view of human nature, 122, 183n.44; compared to inquisitorial system, 115; conception related to rules for conduct, 129–132; justifies special ethic for attorneys, 3, 63n.2; no single conception of, 110

Aristotle: view on moral education strengthened with role modeling, 148–149

Attorney: *See* Legal profession

Autonomy: as element of a profession, 89–91

Bandura, Albert: insights on role models useful for theory of human nature and ethics, 153–156

Bar associations: significance for legal profession, 101–103

Bayles, Michael: domain of legal ethics, xii; regulation of professionals, 180n.70; use of continuum for understanding profes-

sions, 71

Business: distinguished from profession, 83–86

Camenisch, Paul: grounds professional ethics in community values, 165n.16, 175–176n.19

Codes of ethics: element of profession, 93–95, 179n.50, 179n.51, 179n.54; evolving nature of lawyers' codes, 9–12, 165n.23; ground for thinking professionals have special ethics, 3; part of social contract, 179n.50

Confidentiality: ground for distinguishing professional from general ethics, 4; in legal ethics, 13; major problem area for attorneys, 10, 109; roots in adversary system, 109–110; treatment in legal and general ethics, 2

Conflict of interest: main problem area for attorneys, 10, 109; roots in adversary system, 109–110; treatment in legal and general ethics, 6

189

Legal Profession *(continued)* required of attorneys, 99; relation of knowledge and ethics for understanding essence, 175n.19; roles leading to wrongdoing, 180n.70; service, 100–103; whether worthy of respect, 104–106. *See also* Profession(s)

Legal system: similarities with legal ethics and ethical system, 19–21

Levi, Edward: developmental nature of legal process, 20

Lewis, C.I.: attempt to wed Kantianism and utilitarianism, 23–24; development of his view of humans as rule-guided, 56–59; pragmatic features of his ethics, 29–31

Luban, David: attorney as moral agent, 15

Modeling: *See* Role modeling.

Moral Education: as part of universal ethic, 157–158; role modeling implicit in theories of, 146–157, 186n.15

Obligations: *See* Conflicting obligations; Social obligations

Ordinary ethics: *See* General ethics; Universal ethics

Paternalism: governing relationship between professional and client/patient, 87–88; criticized in lawyer-client relationship, 177n.41

Peters, R.S.: view on moral education strengthened with role modeling, 151–152

Piaget, Jean: depicts conduct as rule-guided, 54–55

Plato: moral education, 146–148

Postema, Gerald: calls for flexibility in thinking about professional role, 173n.38

Pound, Roscoe: features of professions, 79–80, 89–90, 101–103

Pragmatic ethical theory: alternatives for conceiving, 27–34; common features, 28; essence applied to legal ethics, 34–35

Pragmatism: approach of lawyers to ethics, xvii; general features useful for understanding nature of legal ethics, 27; view of this book distinguished from, 161. *See also* James, William; Dewey, John; Lewis, C. I.; Pragmatic ethical theory

Pro bono work: related to conception of society, 132–134

Profession(s): autonomy, 89–91, 178n.44, 178n.47, 179n.50; codes of ethics and professional associations, 93–95, 179n.50, 179n.51, 179n.54, 180n.70, conception of suggests rules for conduct, 76; constructing view of, 68–69, 75–95; distinguished from business, 83–86; use of continuum for understanding, 70–73; knowledge, 79–83; 175n.19, 176n.28; law as a profession, 98–106; leadership, 91–93, 178g n.47; methodologies for defining, 67–75, 174n.5, 174n.7; relationship between professional and client/patient, 87–89, 177n.41, 178n.43; relevance of study of professions for nonprofessional, 95–96; service, 83–86; 177n.36; 175–176n.19; significant features as material for construction of professional role, 75–98; special obligations,

Utilitarianism *(continued)*
Gilligan's attempts to avoid, 26;
rule utilitarianism as foundation
for general and professional
ethics, 164n.14

Wasserstrom, Richard: criticizes
paternalism in lawyer-client
relationship, 177n.41

Zealous representation: main problem area for lawyers, 10,
109–110; ways of figuring into
conception of adversary system,
117–121